"This remarkable book shares Alex's lived experience of a rare type of meningioma and the perplexing effects that dramatically altered her sense of reality and control over her thoughts, behaviour, speech and body. Part I charts her journey spanning life prior to the illness, symptom onset and diagnosis, treatment, experience of psychosis, rehabilitation and adjustment to the new normal. Part II is written by a leading neurosurgeon and a world-renowned clinical neuropsychologist and provides the clinical context for understanding Alex's illness and the rehabilitation that was integral to her recovery. Over time, Alex has managed to put the pieces of the puzzle together to find meaning in her illness with the support of family, friends and professionals. This beautifully written, candid and touching account will appeal to other people and family members affected by neurological conditions and cancer, and will inspire anyone facing major life challenges."

Tamara Ownsworth, School of Applied Psychology,
Griffith University, Australia

Life After a Rare Brain Tumour and Supplementary Motor Area Syndrome

This book offers a personal insight into the experience of Alex Jelly, a professional fundraiser who developed a rare brain tumour, a papillary meningioma, which was successfully removed. She was left with Supplementary Motor Area Syndrome and associated problems including motor and speech impairments and a temporary psychosis. Discussing Alex's struggles and triumphs throughout her rehabilitation, this book offers an honest account of her journey from diagnosis to recovery.

Part I introduces Alex's early life and employment, symptom onset and diagnosis, treatment and rehabilitation. Part II presents her neurosurgeon, Adel Helmy, and a clinical neuropsychologist, Barbara A. Wilson. Adel provides a medical context by explaining Alex's successful surgery and her post-operative experience. Finally, Barbara concludes with a comprehensive view of Alex's recovery and gives a voice to the therapists and psychologists who worked with Alex throughout her inpatient and outpatient rehabilitation journey.

This book provides support, understanding and hope for patients who have suffered a brain tumour, and their families. It is valuable reading for any professional involved in neurorehabilitation, students of clinical neuropsychology and those touched by brain injury.

Alex Jelly was a professional fundraiser for charities for many years in London and then a fundraising consultant for UK and international charities. In the summer of 2016 she started to feel odd and that led to the discovery of a brain tumour, which has in turn led to this book.

Adel Helmy is a University Lecturer in the Division of Neurosurgery, University of Cambridge, and an Honorary Consultant Neurosurgeon at Cambridge University Hospitals NHS Trust.

Barbara A. Wilson is a clinical neuropsychologist who has worked in brain injury rehabilitation for 42 years. She has won many awards for her work, including an OBE for services to rehabilitation and five lifetime achievement awards.

After Brain Injury: Survivor Stories
Series Editor: Barbara A. Wilson

With this series, we hope to expand awareness of brain injury and its consequences. The World Health Organization has acknowledged the need to raise the profile of mental health issues (with the WHO Mental Health Action Plan 2013–20) and we believe there needs to be a similar focus on psychological, neurological and behavioural issues caused by brain disorder, and a deeper understanding of the importance of rehabilitation support. Giving a voice to these survivors of brain injury is a step in the right direction.

Published titles:

The Invisible Brain Injury
Cognitive Impairments in Traumatic Brain Injury, Stroke and other Acquired Brain Pathologies
Aurora Lassaletta

My Life with MS, Bipolar and Brain Injury
Living in the Moment
Charlie Bacchus and Marie Beau

Family Experience of Brain Injury
Surviving, Coping, Adjusting
Jo Clark-Wilson and Mark Holloway

Rebuilding Life after Brain Injury
Dreamtalk
Sheena McDonald, Allan Little and Gail Robinson

For more information about this series, please visit: www.routledge.com/After-Brain-Injury-Survivor-Stories/book-series/ABI

Life After a Rare Brain Tumour and Supplementary Motor Area Syndrome

Awake Behind Closed Eyes

Alex Jelly, Adel Helmy and Barbara A. Wilson

Routledge
Taylor & Francis Group

LONDON AND NEW YORK

First published 2020
by Routledge
2 Park Square, Milton Park, Abingdon, Oxon OX14 4RN

and by Routledge
52 Vanderbilt Avenue, New York, NY 10017

Routledge is an imprint of the Taylor & Francis Group, an informa business

British Library Cataloguing-in-Publication Data
A catalogue record for this book is available from the British Library

Library of Congress Cataloging-in-Publication Data
A catalog record has been requested for this book

ISBN: 978-0-367-08540-7 (hbk)
ISBN: 978-0-367-08542-1 (pbk)
ISBN: 978-0-429-02296-8 (ebk)

Typeset in Times New Roman
by Wearset Ltd, Boldon, Tyne and Wear

This book is dedicated to the memory of Polly Higgins, a friend who died tragically and suddenly of cancer at the age of just 50, while this book was being written. Polly was an inspirational champion for the Earth, a barrister who researched, drafted and campaigned for an international crime of ecocide. She did not survive to see this law put into practice but it now, thanks to her work and vision, has every hope of becoming a reality.

Contents

Preface

This book is one of the Survivor Stories, a series of books which offers a personal insight into the experience of a survivor of brain injury. This one tells the story of Alex, a professional fundraiser, who developed a rare brain tumour, a papillary meningioma, which was successfully removed. Alex was left with SMA (Supplementary Motor Area) Syndrome. This syndrome can occur after neurosurgery for a lesion in the SMA. Clinical symptoms can vary from none to a global impairment of voluntary movement, with preserved muscle strength and loss of speech. Typically, these symptoms completely resolve within weeks to months, leaving only a disturbance in alternating bimanual movements.

We learn about Alex's early life and employment together with the early signs that something was wrong. Her neurosurgeon tells us about the successful surgery and the post-operative journey. Alex recalls her early problems including motor and speech impairments and a temporary psychosis. We hear about the neuropsychological rehabilitation she received at the Oliver Zangwill Centre in Ely near Cambridge and her gradual return to health. We learn about Alex's struggles and triumphs along the way and the main messages she wants to give to readers of the book.

Part I of the book is about Alex and her story while Part II by her neurosurgeon Adel Helmy and a clinical neuropsychologist, Barbara A. Wilson, provides background information on meningiomas and Supplementary Motor Area Syndrome, together with reports from people who worked with Alex during her recovery and rehabilitation.

Note: Please note that Alex's story illustrates her perceptions at the time and her views do not necessarily represent those of other patients, the care staff or the clinical practice.

Acknowledgements

Alex would like to thank all her family and friends who have seen her through this time. She sends special thanks to her surgeon, Mr Adel Helmy, and also to her neuro-oncologist, who prefers not to be named, and all the dedicated staff on the ICU, A ward and Lewin Unit at Addenbrooke's, with particular thanks to the hugely committed and capable staff at the Brain Injury Rehabilitation Trust (BIRT) and the Oliver Zangwill Centre, both in Ely. And, of course, to my fabulous, untiring editor, Professor Barbara Wilson, without whom this book would never have been written.

We would all like to acknowledge and thank Mick Wilson for his insightful comments and proofreading of the book and Jessica Fish for her comments and help with references. Thanks, too, for all those who have given permission for their names and reports to be used.

Foreword

As lead psychologist at the Oliver Zangwill Centre for Neuropsychological Rehabilitation (OZC) from 2010 to 2018, I had the opportunity to get to know personally many people whose lives were suddenly and unexpectedly disrupted by a life-altering brain injury. Our mission was to support and accompany these people on their journeys from experiencing the brain injury as a central defining and damaging event in their lives, to putting the injury and its consequences in the background and moving on to recapture their confidence and enjoyment of life, albeit with some quirks and new ways of doing things. This book captures one such journey from the perspectives of survivor Alex, her neurosurgeon, and her psychologists and therapists.

Readers of this latest book in the Survivor Stories series will learn about Alex's full and fascinating life before her diagnosis with a papillary meningioma, a rare and cancerous brain tumour. They will hear her tales of experiencing early post-surgery life when she was unable to communicate her thoughts and her surreal interpretations of the world around her. Her neurosurgeon, Mr Adel Helmy, contributes a clearly written chapter on brain tumours, adding a vital piece of knowledge so the reader can start putting Alex's experience into a medical context. Finally, we hear from the therapists and psychologists who worked with Alex throughout her inpatient and outpatient rehabilitation journey; their voices as given to us by Professor Barbara Wilson round out a comprehensive view of Alex's recovery.

There is something very special about a book that narrates a personal journey through brain injury and beyond. And when that story is told with wit and intelligence, it is even more special. Add to this a professional understanding and explanation of the disease and its progress and rehabilitation, and you have a very full story of the inner workings of an injured brain on its road to recovery. The Survivor Stories series has offered a wealth of insight and knowledge about life with a brain injury from the perspectives of the survivors and their health teams as well as clues to the impact of rehabilitation on recovery and eventual adjustment. In particular, the series, and this book, highlights the value of neuropsychological rehabilitation in helping the injured person not only learn cognitive strategies but also gain a true understanding of their brain and the consequences of damage to it. Good neuropsychological rehabilitation helps people regain their own unique sense of identity and confidence in themselves as whole people, even with an injured brain. Alex's story gives us a rich sense of who she is as a person, her strong values and passions, her determination, and her use of a vast range of resources as she glues the pieces of herself back together again.

As one of the authors of the original Survivor Stories book, I was delighted to read this newest addition to the series. I know Alex personally from her time at the Oliver Zangwill Centre, and I can attest to her bright and curious mind, her determination and persistence, and her wry sense of humour. Her stories of her early days after surgery when she misperceived and misunderstood things around her are filled with humour, but also poignantly help us understand how incredibly difficult, lonely, puzzling and scary these experiences were for her. All of us who routinely encounter patients in their early days will surely have enhanced empathy and understanding for these patients.

One of Alex's most striking experiences in the early days was to misinterpret the world around her and this resulted in anecdotes such as this one:

> I thought at one point that I was the first human in all of history to consciously create HGH or Human Growth Hormone. We all produce it naturally or our pituitary gland does, especially when we're babies and children, but it slows down in production from middle age. I could feel the HGH pulsing through my arms at night, like blood.
>
> I then "realised" that the bags of liquid feed that were delivered through the NG tube contained HGH, and that nurses were trading this (in other words stealing from the hospital and selling it to a range of private individuals who wanted immortality) as bags were always going missing and nurses could never find them when they wanted them.

Alex's neurosurgeon, Mr Helmy, writes a very cogent clinical description of brain tumours, putting Alex's experience within the wider context of this potentially devastating diagnosis: a brain tumour is at once life threatening and also damaging to the very organ we use to cope with life's challenges, the brain. Both lay readers and health professionals will appreciate the clear and straightforward description of the various types of brain tumours and their management.

Professor Wilson adds the voices of the various therapists and psychologists who worked with Alex throughout her journey. It is fascinating to compare their views on Alex's disturbed thoughts and behaviour with her own description of how she felt and thought at the time. The weaving together of the patient experience and the professional outlook and care gives a uniquely well-rounded picture of the injured brain and its healing.

Jill Winegardner, PhD
Director of Neuropsychological Rehabilitation, University Hospitals, Cleveland, USA (formerly lead clinical psychologist, Oliver Zangwill Centre, Ely, UK)

Part I

Alex's story

Chapter 1

Life before

Alex Jelly

I come from a loving, supportive family, the middle of three daughters all separated by about two years in age. As a child I went to the local school, then a convent a little further away, where I travelled by school bus each day, then by my own choice to a boarding school from 16 to 18. I was always happy at school, did well academically and was relatively popular – at least, I never had to make much effort to make friends. My father commented when I was a teenager that I didn't seem to need people and maybe that's why people gravitated towards me – like cats, who always seem to go to whoever *doesn't* like cats!

I graduated in English Literature from York University in 1995 (it was the only subject I was really good at) and after training took a job as an English teacher in Malaysia for two years. I was originally recruited for a school in Beijing, but they faxed me a couple of weeks before I was due to leave (with warm clothes packed) and said they'd just opened a school in Borneo and needed me there for three months. I just needed to repack for a tropical climate and I was ready to go. I loved it there in Malaysia so much that I never did end up going to China.

On return to the UK, when I was ready for a new job, I knew I wanted to work in international development. After some years of international travel, including a month in Malawi when I was 17 (I know, I was lucky; most people's school trips consist of a field trip to the local town!), I could already see the value in skill sharing and wanted to give something back. But the only way into international development was to spend time "in the field", which I hadn't done.

I looked around for a job that would suit an English Literature graduate with, by this time, three years' experience of teaching English, and found a voluntary job as a fundraiser as a first step into the charity world. That was it; I was hooked. I worked in a pub part time to pay the rent for my tiny room in a London flat share and worked for three days a week at a drugs and alcohol charity in London. It turned out to be a stepping stone not to international development but to fundraising, as I then moved to environmental charities and to a couple of fundraising consultancies, working with a number of UK and international clients at any one time. I found fundraising so fulfilling that I couldn't imagine doing anything else. As part of my work at one of the fundraising consultancies, I worked for The Skinners Company, one of the oldest livery companies in London, and for the RSA (Royal Society for the Encouragement of Arts, Manufactures and Sciences), running fundraising campaigns for £2 million and £20 million respectively. Life has always happened to me in the most delightful way. I've never been a planner. A boyfriend (and several friends) used to ask me how I could not have a plan and I would say "life happens"! To be honest I think I was more in love with the glamour of being a fundraiser and with raising money for things I cared about than with the work itself.

I then went travelling for a year in Central America, where I learned (bad) Spanish, and to India, where I learned about yoga in its wider sense – "it's more than just Indian gymnastics", as my London yoga teacher and friend, Kate Douglas, used to say – and had my first introduction to meditation, which for me was a very good experience. I dived in at the deep end with a five-day silent retreat called Z-Meditation, where practitioners stop the thoughts as they occur and then work out the untruth at the core of each, which appealed to my rational side. "$I + X = happiness$" was the core formula we were trying to disprove. So much of our unhappiness or discontent is based around this formula that most of us believe when we say to ourselves: "When I have this or the other, or do this or that, I'll be happy." We know this cannot be true. In fact, when we get the thing we've been craving, whether a new car, house, job or partner, we move on to the next thing or experience that is now supposed to guarantee our happiness.

In India I was very focused on the brain. I heard from several backpackers about a retreat called Vipassana, which was a 10-day silent retreat offered for free all around the world, but I thought this was just another ego-driven, prove-yourself-hard experience. I later did this retreat in Switzerland and the UK and it definitely isn't ego-driven. For example, a longstanding knee problem was resolved in one particular meditation session on my first Vipassana retreat, confirmed by my chiropractor back in London whom I'd been seeing for some time and who said, "This is the first time we haven't had to work on your knee." Experiencing became believing and I gradually (mostly) balanced my belief system to include the body and mind in its widest sense.

I had "discovered" Reiki healing in much the same way in Australia several years before. I was in an outdoor market, on my own, when I saw a sign with a word I'd never heard before. I went up to the stallholder and asked what it was. He said his wife was the "Reiki Master", which sounded quite pretentious to me, but that she was busy right now and could I wait? He would give me a free five minutes while I waited. I agreed, more out of curiosity than anything else, and sat down on the stool he offered. We were in plain view of everyone passing but I did as he asked and closed my eyes. He put his hands near my head and I felt this tremendous wave of heat travel across my skull and down into my neck. "But he isn't even touching me!" I thought. How could this happen? I asked him and he just said it was "energy". If he or anyone else had described it to me I wouldn't at that time have believed them, but experiencing it directly for myself was quite a different matter and served to convince me.

When I decided I didn't want to work for the fundraising consultancy any more I resigned with nothing to go on to. I became friendly with a woman named Polly Higgins, who at the time was setting up a campaign which was to become "Eradicating Ecocide". I found this very exciting, having always cared deeply about the environment, and loved what she was doing. When I discovered Schumacher College near Totnes in Devon and was enticed by their MSc in Holistic Science, I was reluctant as I wanted to stay in London to help Polly, but I did go in the end and what a blessing that was. Not only was it one of the most enriching years of my life intellectually and soulfully, but it was also the place I met my partner, Mike, one of the mainstays of my support system throughout this whole process. In fact, he was an integral part of the Schumacher experience. Schumacher opened me up to the possibilities of life and helped me realise that if you follow a thread of passion, even if you can't see where it's going, it will be rewarding in a way that you can't even imagine. My year group did a module called "Leading in the Midst of Complexity" and I and others decided it should really be called "Hearing the Call" as you cannot force things that don't want to be forced; it's more about developing your listening skills and responding accordingly.

That's how I ended up training in natural building; I had an urge to get my hands and feet in the earth and I followed it. I joined websites facilitating the exchange of skills and work hours for training, accommodation and food (at the time popular websites were WWOOF – Willing Workers on Organic Farms – and Workaway). I worked for week or so at a time doing things like scribing round poles to square cladding, working with earth building and joining a team for a month in France to build a roundhouse. I then joined Straw Works' School of Natural Building, where I met all sorts of interesting people and developed skills in natural materials such as straw, cob, wood and lime. I learned that I could actually *do* this, sort of, with the help and support of others! I had all sorts of dreams of building genuinely affordable as well as sustainable homes and looked for land for a while, but it was never to be. I think now that I was trying too hard to make it into a career, trying to impress other people and straying too far from the "rule" I had already discovered: that if you follow your heart there's really no need to justify it with logical reasons.

Chapter 2

Symptoms and diagnosis
The Lime in the Coconut

Alex Jelly

Looking back I would say it was mid- to late-2016 that the symptoms started to appear, although at the time I didn't put them together. I grew increasingly tired and started to lose weight but put it down to the eco-retrofit I was doing on our house at the time. Early mornings and late nights took the blame. By Christmas I was admitting to my family that I thought I was suffering from depression, something that really scared me as I'd never had it before. The only good thing about this was that I started building a team around me, something that was to stand me in good stead later on. I found a wonderful homeopath, who I still see, went to one meeting with a psychotherapist, which I'd never done before, and invested in some books about this mystery world of depression.

Every time I had a headache or vomited I would put it down to food poisoning, a "bug" or something else. I remember a few days after Christmas 2016, Mike and I were staying in Camber Sands in Sussex and walked into Rye for a massage – it was going to be a lovely treat, but I threw up in the reception area!

I've also recently realised that the pains in my head every time I ventured onto a trampoline with children (for several years before the diagnosis) were a symptom of the brain tumour. It felt like something weighty was being thrown around in the top of my head, but I just put it down to age and long periods between practice on the trampoline. It was not until I joined my nieces on their trampoline in May 2019 and it didn't hurt that I made that connection!

One Monday morning in January 2017 I woke up and vomited into the bin beside our bed (which has holes in the bottom so it seeped slowly into the carpet). I said to Mike that I'd better stay in bed, but he didn't think I was making much sense in my replies to him (and not caring about the carpet!) so he called the GP. When the GP spoke to me and found the same – a delay between questions and then confused-sounding answers – he advised going to the Accident and Emergency (A&E) department. I thought it a bit over the top, but what could I do? We were lucky to live in Cambridge, about a 15-minute drive from one of the best hospitals in the UK, Addenbrooke's, with one of the best neuro units, so off we went, with Mike driving.

The funny thing is that my perception of the conversations with both my partner and the GP that morning was that I could easily have responded more quickly if someone with less patience had forced me to. I thought of my sister's no-nonsense approach and thought, "She wouldn't let me get away with it!" The phrase that was going through my head when Mike or the GP spoke to me was, "Narrow window of opportunity, Jel" (Jel's the name my friends use for me and I sometimes call myself). I was quite bemused by the fact that no words were coming out, even though I knew what I wanted to say and was almost laughing at myself.

At A&E we were seen fairly quickly and some basic details were taken. I remember Mike doing most of the talking with me answering some of the more basic questions. I had started to feel better by then and remembered to cancel an appointment for that day. But they scanned me and came back with the news that I had a growth in my brain and they wanted to keep me in for further checks. I think I vomited in the waiting room – I can't remember that far back. I remember one nurse (or was she a doctor?) breaking the news to me with tears in her eyes, which bemused me still further. I was a healthy and until quite recently happy, fit, 40-something-year-old. What could possibly go wrong? It was exciting to be in hospital with all that attention, but really, what could go wrong with my perfect life?

They kept us in for a couple of nights, with Mike sleeping on the floor of the side room. My younger sister, Debs, came to visit for the meeting on the second day where the surgeon was to explain what kind of growth it was and what their recommendations were for what to do about it. I think I expected an operation at the worst and probably not even that – "Oh, just keep an eye on it, come back for regular scans but nothing to worry about." I couldn't have been more wrong. Mr Helmy brought in a small crew of junior doctors attending, to break the news that I had a tumour about five to six centimetres across ("about the size of a lime") that I had already been told was a bilateral parafalcine meningioma. I leapt on the word "parafalcine", mistakenly believing it to mean "false".

Debs took copious notes, while we were free to listen – an invaluable service and the first of many, and the conversation went something like this:

HELMY: "So you've got a large tumour growing in the middle of your head. I suggest operating fairly soon but it's your choice."

ME: "But you're not worried about it, are you?"

HELMY: "Well, we are keen to take it out."

ME: "But you said it was my choice. What happens if we don't remove it?"

HELMY: "It would continue growing and pressing on the brain, your symptoms would get worse and worse and you'd probably be dead in two months."

So not much choice then. Obviously I agreed to him taking it out, with great faith in his skills as a surgeon, which he wasn't to let down. I asked whether it was a straightforward operation and he explained what he would do but said it was a large tumour and that a brain operation is always a risk. But it was more risky to leave it to grow. I wondered whether it could have been connected with my childhood febrile convulsions, which at one stage had put me in a coma for two days. He said the technology wasn't available in the 1970s to determine whether there was already a tumour, but that it could have been there for 10 years or more. I actually felt glad about the technology not being good enough to identify a tumour in my childhood. Life would have been very different for me knowing that I had a tumour or even a possibility of one – always looking over my shoulder, always being looked out for. I could just imagine the restrictions.

Meanwhile my partner, my beloved Mike, along with Debs, was already doing a sterling job of keeping the family updated as he was to do with an increasingly large circle of friends over the next year (thank you WhatsApp and Teamup apps).

Mr Helmy told me it was almost certainly benign and that I'd be in hospital perhaps for five days or more depending on my recovery. It shocked me when he said I should count on taking the rest of the year for recovery, although in my optimistic state I thought "that won't be me!" He did warn us at this meeting or the next that I might develop a rare condition called SMA Syndrome, which would have stroke-like symptoms and make me paralysed and possibly mute but that it would resolve itself quickly if it did occur. I think I remember my sister looking it up and showing it to me between this meeting and the operation, but this may not have happened. My memory was affected by a process called confabulation – putting different memories together and thinking that they happened together. At any rate, she doesn't share this memory and I never found the web page that I remember looking at with her. But I know it was true that Mr Helmy told us that it might be a possibility as I had a yoga nidra meditation CD that contained the words, "You can move your body but you're choosing to not move your body." I listened to this before the operation and remember thinking how useful this meditation would be if I were paralysed. I was thinking it but I didn't believe it would actually happen. I've also recently found a note in my handwriting in the early days, before I could speak, referring to SMA Syndrome.

The few weeks between this and the operation were filled with visits from friends, walks, pubs, meals out, consulting friends with nutritional and personal training backgrounds to see what I should be eating and doing in preparation for an operation as I'd been losing weight. They were fun weeks but with a slight sense of trepidation. I remember one particular swim in the local pool where I stopped in the middle of a lane and burst into silent tears at the thought of not being able to do this again – what if I *were* paralysed by this and could never again feel my body moving so smoothly through the water? It almost happened but I'm glad to say (spoiler alert!) that a few months later I was swimming again.

Mike and I called the tumour "The Lime in the Coconut" because we'd recently been introduced to a Caribbean song about Da Lime and da Coconut but later when I realised it was malignant I resisted giving it a name as I thought it would make me subconsciously fond of it and therefore liable to hang on to it.

Chapter 3

The op
Happy Valentine's Day

Alex Jelly

The operation was scheduled for Tuesday 14 February 2017 – happy Valentine's Day! I was prepared, bag packed for five days, armed with goodies that friends had sent, including frankincense for my pillow, eye masks aplenty, pyjamas and tops with generous necks to get over my head gently after the head operation, crystals, and a wooden statue of Ganesha, the Indian elephant god, remover of obstacles. A friend had given me a hand-painted picture of Ganesha, but it was too big to bring and anyway I thought I'd see it in just a few days.

I had spoken to a friend of a friend who had had a brain tumour and the operation to remove it and I thought I was clued up, but she'd been in and out in a few days, so it was entirely irrelevant except her advice not to wear nail varnish (because one of the signs the medical team looks for during the operation is whether your fingers are losing colour) and to 'put your big girl pants on'. How ignorant I now know I was to think that all brain tumours are the same or even similar.

My parents had asked if they could visit me in hospital and at first I'd said no, it was too much hassle for them to travel, I'd be out in five days and Mike wouldn't want them staying at our house in the midst of such turmoil. In the end they booked a hotel, saying they would come anyway and I was so glad they did. They came to visit in the hospital on the Thursday and were two of my first visitors.

Obviously I don't remember anything about the operation but I do remember Mike driving us to the hospital early in the morning and waiting a long time before being seen, meanwhile being called in occasionally for MRSA swabs and the like. I also remember sitting in bed waiting for the operation. I'd had to have a shower in antibacterial lotion and wash my hair with the same stuff – it was horrible and did my hair no good at all! But it was necessary to stop infection.

I'll let Mike and Mr Helmy tell the rest. Their descriptions are in Part II.

Chapter 4

Early visits

Alex Jelly

Mike was my first visitor and after him my parents and sisters. Shockingly for us all, I had woken up unable to move or talk. After some time I was able to write. Cat, my older sister, would test me on my memory and I would write down the answers. She was lovely and supportive but I thought she was a fool and wrote so, as it was blindingly obvious to me that I could remember everything – but how was she to know?

Debs, my younger sister, seemed to know I was in there all along. She was the one who helped me to speak for the first time by singing parts of songs and having me complete them. When I found out that they all started with or contained the same first line – "There was I" – I began to think that this was another conspiracy – something around drugs, I thought. So much of our childhood entertainment in the Seventies was produced under the influence of drugs after all. *The Magic Roundabout,*[1] for example, a programme that I remember watching regularly, has been described as "a coded manifesto for the Sixties drug culture" ("Matt", 2001).

The copper-bottomed guarantee

My father had said from the beginning that he was giving me a "copper-bottomed guarantee" that I would survive this. I had never heard of the expression, which refers to the most expensive wooden ships being given a copper bottom that almost guaranteed they would only suffer minimal damage and would also speed across the water faster than their rivals. I had read that copper can build up in the brain and lead to Alzheimer's. I thought this meant that I would develop Alzheimer's – or that he would. A woman whom I will call V, who was on the A ward with me, had some kind of dementia and I dreaded it. It scared the bejesus out of me every time he said it! It was only when I was well enough to talk and to make myself understood that he explained the expression.

I thought I was a seer in those early days. When my father came to visit once when I was on the Lewin Rehabilitation Unit, I told him there were patients who would shout out at night and seemed to be prescient (this is detailed in my short stories *Nein, nein, nein!* and *Drugs* later on). When the nurse on duty that morning asked whether I had slept well, I had written down, "No ... a mental patient was shouting in the next ward", and I remember the nurse correcting me, "not mental – special needs".

My dad asked whether I thought I was a seer and I said yes. He then asked me if I knew how he would die and when I said yes he asked me how. I immediately said "Parkinson's or Alzheimer's", partly because of his copper-bottomed guarantee, partly because I remember him telling us how his mother had dementia before she died. He seemed to take this in and consider it carefully, not laughing at me, which is absolutely the right way, I learned, to be with people who are delusional. He continues to be one of my greatest teachers, though he's 81 at the time of writing. We call him the Old Goat, but he's a wise young thing!

When my mother visited on her own, for the first few visits she would bring me photos of me on family holidays or with friends to jog my memories. She also brought cheese and salad cream sandwiches on white bread – it used be on Mighty White bread with the crusts cut off – which was a childhood meal with tomato soup when we were ill. When she realised I immediately recognised all the people and places in the photos she knew I was "in there" and stopped bringing them. She continued to bring the sandwiches though and I loved them, even though they tasted a little dry to me (as all food did then). I just loved the memory of them and the fact that she brought them.

Emilie and Evandro came to visit me fairly early on. Evandro is a friend of Mike's and is Brazilian. Emilie was his partner (now his wife) and is French. Mike said later that Evandro had been one of his most constant friends through the whole period of my hospitalisation. They are now good friends of mine and I was really disappointed to have to miss their wedding that summer but I just couldn't have handled it. Anyway, they came to visit, with Evandro obviously emotional, tears in his eyes, and Emilie holding it together (she later told me she saved her tears for outside the hospital). They brought a bouncy ball on one of their later visits when I had regained control over my arms and hands. The game we played was that you would drop (or throw) the ball on the floor, it would bounce up and the next person would catch it and bounce it back. When it came to my turn I found myself completely unable to drop it; it must have been something to do with not being able to initiate movement. I could take it in my hands and even catch it but I couldn't let go! I knew I was progressing when I started to be able to throw it, and I even practised with my left hand, which I got quite good at.

Dehydration

I was always thirsty in those early days. It seemed I could never get enough water. I had to drink from a teaspoon because I didn't have the necessary muscle control in my lips to sip from a glass. I understand now why babies have to suckle and why they dribble when first offered a cup. Mike always somehow intuited my needs and would offer me water from a teaspoon, then later a straw, until I was replete. Other patients were not so lucky and I remember telling one patient's visitor that she was dehydrated. The visitor replied that her friend had water by the bed. She couldn't prop herself up, let alone reach out for the beaker of water! But I was far from being able to articulate this or even realise it at the time.

Catheters

Catheters drain into a bottle or bag and it seemed mine was always full. Nurses did come round to empty them, but at times you could be left for hours and a full catheter bag is really uncomfortable, especially when you have a urine infection as I did (I came into hospital with one). I remember a lovely Italian nurse telling a more senior nurse that I needed my catheter changing although the date on it wasn't up yet – apparently she'd learnt that you needed to allow less time in certain circumstances – and thankfully the senior nurse took it well from her junior instead of getting in a huff, saying something about always learning. This is before I could speak and I was so grateful because it was getting horribly itchy.

I remember another time – at night – when I thought nurses were making a pantomime of emptying the bag and the patients in my ward were in on it too. I'd told Mike that day (probably either in a whisper or in writing) that my catheter needed emptying and asked him to have a word with the nurses for me. It felt like they were mocking me that night but they probably (or certainly) weren't. It was more likely to be another hallucination. It's fascinating to me now to realise how many of our perceptions are based on what we've already thought, as if to confirm them. It must be a form of confirmation bias. I want to make it clear that these are my own perceptions, or misperceptions, and in no way reflect on the standard of nursing care.

Body dysmorphia

I remember seeing nurses and even the slimmest looked wonderfully healthy and plump. I remember gazing at their arms which, compared to mine, were so meaty! I envied them this as I was so skinny at the time and some of them used to comment on it. One nurse in particular used to describe to her companion while they were giving me a bed bath how her boyfriend described her as an "Oompa Loompa" as she was a bit chubby and how she'd love to be as tiny as me. I thought rather the other way around: that I would love to be well rounded, like her.

I also thought that other people – nurses usually – were variously fat or thin versions of themselves. This was probably just that I was getting nurses mixed up in the early days and thinking two different-sized nurses were the same person. But there was so much talk of losing weight among the nurses on the ward – "Have you seen X? She's put on such a lot of weight! She must have really pigged out on holiday!" or "Have you seen Y? She's so skinny! She thinks she looks amazing but I think she looks anorexic!"

Pets and gardening featured highly on the list of topics of conversation among staff too; I suppose these are topics that most people can join in with. But at the time I read these conversations – that I was "obviously" supposed to hear – as messages to get a pet or take up gardening. Once, much later on, while we were walking in the Magog Hills near Cambridge, we met a man out walking his dogs. He told us he worked as a gardener and was proud of doing so as he was in his 70s. This proved it to me – that both dogs and gardening were the key to longevity and maybe even immortality. I used to mention to the nurses whenever I'd been gardening at home as it seemed to get a good reaction, but also partly to prove I was "getting it".

I've been trying to describe what it felt like to be paralysed ... you know the feeling when you've had a local anaesthetic on some part of your body and you can feel movements against your body – the vibrations – but not your actual body part? It felt a bit like that. Or when you're in the deepest meditation state (for example, a body scan meditation) where you've totally let go of all tension. When the nurses would bed bath me or change my nappy (as I always thought of it) I was aware they were moving me but couldn't actually feel any sensations. But really, it's indescribable, unless you've been there, though I do have a somatic memory of it which I can sometimes access.

I do remember looking down at one foot and willing it to move – I amused myself by recalling that Daniel Day Lewis film, *My Left Foot*, and saying to my left foot, in my head, "Move, damn you!" I had managed to wiggle the toes the day before for my family and to my surprise the top of the foot now moved. I was elated! No, that's not true, I'm elated at the *memory* of it. At the time it just seemed normal. I couldn't feel anything as extreme as elation.

I had blood coming from my right nostril and believed it was a brain bleed. I kept picking and picking at it until my friend, Jane, told me that she'd known someone who'd had a nose bleed and kept picking at it until she was taken into hospital for a serious injury to her nose. That scared me into stopping.

It's so hard to describe how I felt back then because everything just *was*.

I do remember feeling isolated and alone every time someone pulled the curtains across my bed – I suppose that's why they left them open at night as well as to do medical checks – but my visitors in the early days must have assumed I wanted privacy. It was particularly felt when my partner or family left. I even remember whispering to my partner (on the A ward, long before I could officially talk) as he left, "Isolation. Despair."

I mistakenly believed – and said to various people along the way – that I had Locked-In Syndrome. I now know, courtesy of Natalie at the BIRT (Brain Injury Rehabilitation Trust) and later Barbara Wilson, via Sarah at the Oliver Zangwill Centre, that I didn't. This is a much more serious condition from which it is rare to recover and it's in a completely different part of the brain. But it is how I felt in those early days, especially before my speech came back and I couldn't move. Every time my curtains were pulled and I was alone, I felt locked in.

Note

1 This was a children's television programme that ran from 1965 to 1977.

Chapter 5

Psychosis and stories
Insights and butterflies

Alex Jelly

Memories of the operation

I believed I had memories of the operation in the first few days following it. I would drift in and out of consciousness and hear and smell things that I believed were real memories. I thought I remembered the gurgling of digestion (probably my own tummy or other patients' in the beds around me) and saw in my mind's eye these massive grey pipes, a view inside my own body as I thought at the time. I saw myself on a huge table in the middle of the bay, being operated on and being asked if I wanted a male or female brain.

I heard my friends urging me to choose one way or another depending on their gender. The particularly feminist voices were strongest. I heard my father, my brother-in-law and Mr Helmy say "Male! Go on, choose male, you know we're the best!" and a female friend arguing "No! Female! We've got the future on our side!" I heard the cackle of witches (probably a group of nurses chatting and laughing) – including my old housemistress, who died years ago but was a really strong role model for me – and I heard loud male voices including Mr Helmy's. They were each trying to persuade me to become male or stay female. I eventually weighed it up and chose female. The women howled with triumph and the male voices faded away but I felt their displeasure.

I could smell the nurses and identify them first by their perfume, then only later by name. It's amazing how the sense of smell developed first, just as it does in babies. Later, a practitioner of Network Spinal Analysis, which I talk about later, reminded me of something I think I'd learned during my MSc dissertation, that the sense of smell is the only sense that passes to the brain directly, unmediated by the thalamus, the mid brain. Most other sensory information gets turned into electric signals first, but smells are received by the brain as the original chemicals – like an amoeba, he said, meaning that an amoeba doesn't translate everything into electric signals.

That's how I came to realise I was going through the same development as I had when I was a baby, but this time I would do it consciously – and maybe even remember it, as indeed I still do. It was fascinating to me at the time and now even more so.

I actually *felt* myself growing in strength night after night and remembered my friend, Bron, the mother of my baby godson, saying that Henry did "night gym", moving around at night in his cot and later pulling himself up on the bars. I would deliberately strengthen my arms on the bars of my bed at night. As I mentioned earlier, I had to drink from a teaspoon because I didn't have the necessary muscle control in my lips to sip from a glass. I understood then why babies have to suckle and why they dribble when first offered a cup. It took a long time to be able to brush my own teeth and even longer to spit, and it took a good while longer than that to learn to yawn. I had seen, shortly before the operation, a YouTube video of a toddler escaping over a wooden indoor fence and climbing out to freedom. I felt a certain affinity with babies and toddlers as I couldn't articulate my thoughts and could only cry or make a harsh sound when upset, disappointed or angry.

Making plans for the future

The nurses used to pull down the TV in front of my bed on the A ward when they had finished giving me a bed bath and leave me in front of it for hours. I suppose it kept patients occupied and quiet and maybe many of them enjoyed it. I definitely didn't but it was so compelling, with all those moving pictures and sounds, that I couldn't tear my eyes away from it, even when Mike or another visitor arrived. It seemed that every programme was being targeted to me personally. There was one I used to watch, *Wanted Down Under*, where couples visited Australia ahead of possible emigration. It seemed like it was a message to me that life was short and that Mike and I should consider moving to another country.

Another programme was about a woman in a wheelchair who was working in fashion and trying to convince fashionable shops to have mannequins in wheelchairs modelling clothes in their windows. She was having quite a bit of success and the programme showed her or the presenter interviewing people on the street to canvass their views on this mannequin in a wheelchair. I thought at this point that I might always be in a wheelchair and that this is what I'd do – campaign for the rights of wheelchair users. It made me feel positive about my future and added to this was the fact that I thought my friend Bron was already in a wheelchair. She's a quite brilliant lawyer so I thought we could set up a campaign together for wheelchair users in professional life.

Another time, much later when I had moved to the Lewin Rehabilitation Unit, I had a meeting with one of the assistant psychologists. She was Italian and I told her I spoke Italian (I don't, beyond a few tourist-style words). When she asked me where I'd learned it I told her I'd had a bar job on Lake Como for a summer and she, of course, believed me. I also said that that's where Mike and I had got engaged. I later thought, "Well, I'm going to make it true and when I'm well again, I'm going to propose to Mike on the shores of Lake Como!" It was more to make conversation and have something to say than lying, though I knew full well it wasn't the truth. The assistant psychologist later asked Debs, my sister, whether it was true and Debs said she couldn't remember me working in Lake Como but it might have happened (we had both travelled so much) but that Mike and I were definitely not engaged.

Interestingly, on the language front, I've just been staying with a friend in Spain who is fluent in Spanish and she reminded me that on her first visit to see me I was talking to her in Spanish. Perhaps it's easier for the brain to think and speak a language that you're not fluent in where it's all just sounds, as opposed to your native language where every word means something.

A friend comes to call

It was Jane! It was really her! In the bed opposite me in hospital! I knew she'd sprained her ankle a few months back but she lived in Totnes – she must have somehow wangled a transfer all the way from Devon to be with me. Jane was one of a group of great friends I had met on a yoga holiday years ago – she had been the yoga teacher on that holiday, in fact. She had been through a tough time emotionally and one of our crew, Karolyne, who is particularly gifted at sending the right thing at the right moment, had made and sent her a silver necklace in the shape of a heart to tell her we all were holding her in our hearts.

She was only there for a couple of days but that was long enough for her to make signs to me to avoid taking the tubed feed (she made signs to pull it out) and to tell me it was her – as if I didn't recognise her! – by making a sign of a heart at her throat. I later "realised" she was trying to make a padlock sign for "locked in".

One of our mutual friends, Mel, was over from Ireland by complete coincidence, visiting other friends in Cambridge so came to visit me in hospital. This was just a few days after the operation, before I could move or speak and it was so frustrating. I kept looking over at Jane's bed and Mike kept saying to Mel, "She's so interested in her neighbours!"

It was like they couldn't see her! I kept wanting to say, "LOOK! IT'S JANE!" but of course couldn't. And of course it wasn't her in ordinary reality. But I believed it was and Jane later said that she had felt so connected with me for those first few days in a much deeper way – and that's how I came to realise psychic presence is a real phenomenon. She had sent me yoga nidra recordings, frankincense essential oil, and other small but meaningful gifts in the weeks leading up to the operation. Later it transpired that frankincense is one of the only substances that passes through the blood–brain barrier, which neither of us knew at the time but which she later found out and sent me a letter about. This meant that it was even more valuable to me as it could cross the barrier that usually keeps everything out and makes it hard to treat the brain.

When she came to visit me in the flesh, I was deeply suspicious of everything and everyone and made her promise to write it all down and report it to my homeopath, Marlow (Jane was also a homeopath). I was so worried that Jane would get murdered on the way home as she had all these secrets about me now and knew I'd have to take the blame if anything happened to my dear friend.

Power

I wielded a certain sort of power, which I enjoyed in a twisted way. I would stare at people quite naturally – it was a certain fixation on moving objects so that I seemed unable to tear my eyes away from people – but I sometimes didn't even try to look away when nurses looked uncomfortable as some of them did when they were washing or dressing me. The phrase that would go through my head was "Oh, the indignity of it all!" and I thought this was in some way payback. But I feel sorry for them now – not only did they have to deal with my bodily fluids and soiled sheets but they had to suffer my death mask too.

Building rapport

In my work as a fundraising consultant I often ran workshops in building rapport with donors. I was naturally good at building rapport anyway (she says modestly) but studying for the teaching these workshops taught me some of the more formal ways of doing it. So the knowledge moved from being ingrained (procedural) to formalised (semantic). I had this obsession with building rapport with the nurses as a key to getting out of hospital. From the earliest days of not being able to move a muscle, I knew I had to develop facial expressions in order to build rapport both with nurses and with friends and family to let them know I was still me. I remember John, a friend from school, who came to visit in the first few days saying "Jel's definitely still in there", when I managed to give him a quizzical – perhaps even scathing – look in response to a question. His girlfriend, Karolyne, who is a close friend quite separately from John, somehow already knew I was in there but it seemed to also confirm it for her.

"People like people who are like them" was one of the things I remembered teaching in the rapport course. I was on the Lewin Unit when I remembered this and it was in response to a situation where I was having a conversation with one of the nutritionists or "food ladies". I had written down that I wanted her to engage me in conversation but had made the mistake of telling her about my flat in Putney where I had lived for years and that was now giving me a rental income. I saw a look cross her face that meant to me that she was thinking we were from different walks of life. I knew I'd have to watch my words if I was to build rapport with her.

Bacteria

I remember a friend sending me a book called *The Freak Brothers* (Figure 5.1), a hardback comic book that was too heavy for me to lift in my weakened state.

I could only turn a few pages and felt that there was some force stopping me reading too far. Anyway, it featured a character, Fat Freddy, a drug addict who had contracted syphilis and was passing it on to his girlfriend and thus to all his friends (as he found out that she was sleeping with most of them). From here developed one of my main stories about bacteria – though syphilis is a virus – and I dreamed on the night before I was moved to the Lewin Unit about bacteria and how clever they are. When I was transferred the next evening to the Lewin I saw my new neighbour opposite me in her bed and thought "That's Fat Freddy!" The cartoon figures in the book all had large, pointy noses and she had a rather large nose too, which was accentuated by the NG tube (naso-gastric tube) plaster.

Fat Freddy was trying to spread syphilis everywhere when he found out that his girlfriend was cheating on him with his friends. This transformed for me into a story in which bacteria were trying to spread everywhere to survive. In turn this hooked in with a story about me being Jewish and wanting a bigger bladder to deal with my UTI – but I realised this would mean having a bigger bowel and bigger digestive system and so on; to

Figure 5.1   The Freak Brothers book.

make a long dream short, it didn't work. The next step was how to escape this blighted body. Brain in a jar story coming up.

In my head at the time all or most men were evil, trying to spread disease to women. My neighbour's husband had been in the Navy before he retired and I was quite convinced that he had come back from one trip with a venereal disease that he passed onto my neighbour (who had ceased, for this time, to be Fat Freddy). I opened several cards that seemed to suggest this, with hints to a time in the past when people had been part of voyages to far lands with prostitutes and venereal diseases (as if we don't have them here!) My neighbour even lent me a magazine with what seemed to be an evil leer, which I was afraid to read lest it had traces of fluid on it that would infect me. My partner became an object for suspicion as well (again – poor Mike!) for similar reasons.

This became quite a theme. I played with my breath, breathing in when I thought that Fat Freddy was trying to spread bacteria through childhood diseases, hundreds of years ago, holding my breath to suffocate the bacteria. I looked in hatred at my poor neighbour, who was totally unaware that I was wishing her (as Fat Freddy) a painful death. She was probably involving me in her own fantasies at the time. I can understand now why patients try to do each other harm in hospitals and mental health care homes, as portrayed in films like *Shutter Island*.

I thought that bacteria were taking over bodies in hospital so that when a patient died and a living body became available, bacteria would take it over and it would seem, to the outside world, that nothing had changed. The person was to all intents and purposes still alive, and friends and family would continue to visit. But it wasn't really them.

Either that or the patient themselves would want to leave the body and become just a brain, as the body really is quite a liability to immortality (ever seen those films where the brain lives forever in a jar?) There were units on the end of each bed that looked like alien versions of brains through my eyes, which were not yet focusing correctly, so when I saw an empty bed where my neighbour should have been with one of these on the pillow I thought, "She's done it! She's made the leap!" She was most likely just at lunch while I was still "eating" from an NG tube and therefore couldn't go to the dining room.

Human Growth Hormone

I thought at one point that I was the first human in all of history to consciously create HGH or Human Growth Hormone. We all produce it naturally or our pituitary gland does, especially when we're babies and children, but it slows down in production from middle age. I could feel the HGH pulsing through my arms at night, like blood.

I then "realised" that the bags of liquid feed that were delivered through the NG tube contained HGH, and that nurses were trading this (in other words stealing from the hospital and selling it to a range of private individuals who wanted immortality) as bags were always going missing and nurses could never find them when they wanted them.

I took my NG tube out early one morning when on the A ward. I don't know why I did it, although I've told people since it was because I was hungry. I think in reality I was influenced by "Jane", mentioned earlier, who I thought was trying to tell me to take it out. I just started pulling it – I think it was blocked at the time – and it started pouring all this delicious fluid into my throat so I kept on. It was surprisingly easy to do – I suppose my muscles were fairly flaccid at the time – so by the time the nurses came to check my blood pressure it was out. Of course, they put another in that day but I was very proud of myself, the way a child would be when they've done something slightly naughty but very grown up. I enjoyed the nurses telling Mike and my family and thought I was very rebellious for doing something that I wasn't supposed to. We have so little power when we're patients!

The sex change

When I arrived on the Lewin Unit I thought I had had a sex change. I had overheard a nurse on A ward call me Jeffrey (probably a mistake – for Jelly) and I was convinced that the woman next to me on the day I arrived on the Lewin was Jeffrey, a man who had had a sex change. Her name was androgynous – what could be more obvious? Also obvious to me was that the patient opposite me had had a sex change (she had a feeding tube plastered to her nose and I thought she'd had rhinoplasty), as had the other woman in my bay, who I thought (almost certainly incorrectly) I had witnessed masturbating as if she had a penis and then whispering "Disgusting" when she caught me looking at her. There wasn't much else to look at in a bay of four people. I thought she was a manifestation of my Great Uncle Aubrey, who had passed away some years ago.

I think I had my period in those few days – I heard a nurse say something about me being "on the rag" as she was washing me, which is a rather coarse expression for menstruating. But at the time I thought that they were trying to convince me I was a woman now – I was supposed to have been a man for goodness' sake! I chose the full version of my name when they asked me what I would prefer to be called as Alex is an androgynous name (Figure 5.2).

One of my visitors must have corrected them as I've not been known by my full name since childhood. Later a nurse would use my full name (Alexandra) – my "Sunday name" we called it – to stop me when I was doing something for too long like brushing my teeth. It worked!

On the sex change note, my assistant neuropsychologist, of whom I've written above, left her timer on my table when she had finished a session one day. I thought she'd left it deliberately when I mistook her handwritten "Marcella" for "Marcello" and thought, "Even Marcella used to be a man!"[1] And there was a nurse whom I will call M, who I also thought had had a sex change because of her name, which was so close to Marcello. I thought they were all clues that were left for me to work out.

There seemed to be a separation too in the Lewin's dining room between men and women, with all the women sitting on one table and all

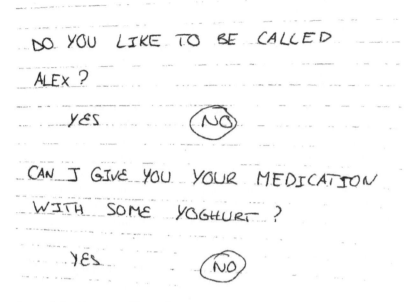

DO YOU LIKE TO BE CALLED

ALEX ?

   YES   (NO)

CAN I GIVE YOU YOUR MEDICATION

WITH SOME YOGHURT ?

   YES   (NO)

Figure 5.2 Alex, not Alexandra.

the men on another for a while. I would very deliberately choose the "women's table" to "prove" that I was really a woman.

I remember my second wheelchair in the Lewin – they had upgraded me to one of the new ones – and looking at the arms. It seemed to me that it was designed for the future, with lots of functions that wouldn't come into play until the time was right. Apart from it coming to a halt at times, which I took to mean that our world wasn't ready for it yet, there were slight circular depressions in the arms of the chair that must have been designed to be buttons later on. I could feel the spaces below the fabric. "Aha!" I thought, "These are for the future. I wonder what they'll do." I imagined them doing all sorts of things, perhaps lifting a fork to the patient's mouth, perhaps squirting water like a clown for a laugh (or a wash or a drink), perhaps even sprouting wings!

Much later, perhaps six weeks before I left Addenbrooke's, I remember being asked to fill in the date board in the dining room on the Lewin. This was offered to me as a "big responsibility but we think you can handle it" when the patient who had previously been doing it left. I thought, "They're trying to keep me in here forever! They're never going to let me out", thinking that they would say I was far too important to be discharged. So initially I said no. But I got on well with the occupational therapist (OT) who'd asked me and so I said yes eventually, on the condition that she do it on days when she was in and I wouldn't be held back because of it. She promised. There were magnets for the day, the month and the year and my "job" was to stick them on the whiteboard every morning so that all the patients knew the date.

As it was, most patients never looked at the board. Sign blindness, it might have been called. I felt as though the signs above the beds were sometimes not read and did not always reflect reality. My friend, Tab, remembers coming to visit when the sign said I was only to be fed pureed food – they served me several blobs on a plate: carrots, mashed potatoes and meat, all shaped and coloured to look like the real thing – though I had been eating solid food by that time. She later told me, "I knew you wouldn't eat that mess, but then you gobbled it all up, really quickly!" I put this down to Environmental Dependence Syndrome, which I describe below. The speed of eating I can't explain as previously I had always been rather a slow eater.

I boasted to the nurses that I used to have two jobs, thinking that I would prove myself to be the hardworking type (as they all worked so hard), another test to pass as I thought. The one was the date board as I've described; the other was gardening – this only involved watering the plants, but I used to make a huge deal out of it. I was officially not allowed into the small kitchen where the tap was located, to fill up the watering cans, but I used to go in there anyway whenever the strictest member of staff was away from the area. Sometimes I got caught but not very often.

My first task was to reorganise the dates – the previous patient had left them in a mess – in the box that was stored with the food supplements, which is another story. I used to write in my journal, "Fill in the date board" and then mark it "Done – success!" in what strikes me now as a rather exaggerated way. But back then, it was the only way to persuade myself to get out of bed and start the day after a usually disturbed night. It actually also helped me to stay in touch with the outside world. And it was then that I started noticing the bags of feed and watching nurses come and take them.

Back on the A ward the nurses used to write the date at the entrance to each bay along with the nurse and health care assistant (HCA) on duty, but sometimes they'd forget and the date would remain unchanged for a few days. From my current perspective, that seems understandable with constantly changing shifts and a busy staff team, but back then I thought someone was slowing down time and messing with my head. What date was it really? How many days had I been here? I was so suspicious! And sometimes I couldn't see the date from where I was lying and I had the bed closest to the door – goodness knows how the other patients kept track.

I totally failed to appreciate that there were set visiting hours, even though my partner had stretched these by charming the heads of wards and the nurses. I had never been in hospital for any period of time and those hours in the morning before visiting hour at lunchtime stretched out forever. I used to think that there were bacteria in the clocks, moving them out of sync, and that during my mini naps they'd get to work, turning the hands back. Once, my partner was 10 minutes late and I just stared at him and then back at the clock. He got the message but poor Mike had had to juggle work meetings, traffic, parking and everything else to get to me!

I would try anything different to see if it would work. I became – as Mike told me later – "more of a scientist than Stephan" in reference to our scientist friend and teacher at Schumacher College, Stephan Harding. "Always experimenting!" Mike would say, and I was. Soup in a bowl, rather than a cup, feet in or out of the bedsheets, a certain moisturiser above another, doing things with my left rather than my right hand, all could make a difference in my mind. I even drew a diagram of lights that were left switched on at night in a neighbouring office across the garden from a side room I was in to see if that would make a difference to my sleeping.

The trouble was, documenting things, especially reasons for waking up, was counter-productive and I ended up with reams of information that only served to keep me awake and to alert the nurses to my actions as my alarm tag would go off whenever I visited the bathroom. It must have been on the outer edge of what I jokingly came to call "my territory". One Sunday evening, after a weekend at home during which I removed my tag, I requested that it be put back on my left hand and was convinced that this made a difference.

Killing my niece

Through a combination of misunderstandings and the psychosis, I believed that it was my destiny as a bacterial colony to kill my niece and become my sister's daughter. I was under the impression that I would invade Tessa's brain as meningitis (most likely influenced by all the talk of meninges and meningiomas) and that she would die but I would take over her body. One day I told my sister I was going to kill her first-born child. She was horrified until she realised what I meant!

That's why, I suppose, whenever I had an "insight" about being a child or how to take care of children, I would pass it on to my sister. If I was going to become her daughter she would need to know! This must have been exhausting for her, having to listen to her (child-free) sister telling her all about parenthood, but she rarely let on.

I thought that I had to be in this situation for some reason and remembered that I'd told my nephew when he had cancer a few years before that I'd do anything – even swap places with him – to save him. At first I thought this was why I was where I was, but when Debs brought the rest of her family on a visit one day and we were playing outside on the lawn of the Jubilee Gardens, Tessa followed a ball right up to the Paediatrics Unit door. I felt instant horror – perhaps it was Tess who was destined to get ill and die! I thought, "Maybe that's why I'm here, to save Tessa!" I was always trying to think of good reasons to be in my situation, either paying something back or preventing something from happening.

Spies

I thought that there were spies everywhere I went. One day I was with my mother in the Jubilee Gardens and we sat on a bench where a nurse was already sitting. I recognised her – she wasn't from my ward but I'd definitely seen her around. When my mother went to get a coffee from inside, I confronted the poor nurse and asked her if she was spying on me. She looked a little bemused and said that she was just enjoying the sunshine and eating her lunch. "Aha!" I thought, "That's exactly what a spy WOULD say!"

Similarly a cleaner on the Lewin Unit was always hanging around where I was, including sitting down right at the door to the garden off the dining room, where I so often was to be found once I could walk, or she would even be sitting on the bench outside. One day, again with my mother visiting, she seemed to be hanging around the door to the side room where I had been moved to a few days before. As my mother and I were inside the room, talking, I became convinced that she was eavesdropping, listening in to our conversation. So I confronted her, asking if she was "spying on me, or something". I tried to make it sound like a joke, but wasn't very good in those days at the subtle intonation that you need to make jokes and I can imagine she knew I was serious. She, of course, denied it and now I realise that it wasn't true.

I even saw one of the patients from my bay a few weeks after she left, sitting in her wheelchair on the concourse and thought *she* was spying on me and was going to report me if I tried to escape. Now I realise she had simply moved wards and was enjoying time on the concourse, but at the time it seemed as if spies were placed all around me.

One day I had an "insight" that anything could be true if you believed in it enough and nothing was if you didn't believe in it. I tested this by having an espresso from Costa on the hospital concourse. Before this, I had "known" that I was super-sensitive to caffeine and wouldn't be able to sleep afterwards. But now – miracle of miracles – it didn't affect me at all. The flip side was that if I didn't believe in my homeopathic remedies they wouldn't work for me. I wanted them to work for me and believed they did. I was made so afraid by this "insight" for this reason, but the insight was only partially true. If you believe you can do something within your physical and mental capacity, you probably can. And you can push yourself outside of your known limits to do something you really want, like running a marathon. We've all heard of people who have been known to exhibit super-human strength in extreme circumstances, for example lifting a car to save a child or person they love.

But of course I was sensitive to caffeine – it was only the drugs and the brain damage and the inevitable sleep deprivation from nights at the hospital that made me sleep despite the espresso. And of course the remedies worked, just as drugs do. No amount of thinking they can't work can block their effectiveness. I do believe that if you're open to such things they work better for you, but to think that they couldn't work at all now seems ridiculous.

I had songs in my mind that I thought were messages. In fact, this has always been the case and I really do believe it's my subconscious sending me messages as I'll wake up with a particular song on my mind that I haven't heard for years and it'll usually be relevant to something.

One such song in the hospital was "Black Velvet" by Alannah Myles. The phrase, "A new religion that'll bring you to your knees ..." kept playing and playing in my mind. My thought was, "But what is this new religion? Is it Buddhism? Is it yoga?" until then I heard a couple of nurses talking about football and I thought, "Of course! It's football! That's the new religion of the day in our culture!"

I thought the televisions and radios were slowing down and speeding up according to which "level" I was on. I had this idea that as I discovered things in hospital I would move up a level in the game and be promoted to a new position. It seemed to me that the TV would respond to this and would speed up with an alarming whoosh of sound. Like when you've been listening to something on a record player and you remove the needle only to set it down at a different point on the record which is going at a different, faster speed. I also thought this about the traffic outside the Lewin Unit – that it would speed up and slow down. I later realised that there was a roundabout just out of sight of the dining room windows at which traffic would slow down at busy times.

I also thought particular friends had particular skills (which of course they do) and that I should ask certain people for certain things within their skill set. So, for example, my sister loves to cook and create new dishes and she cooked for me. My friend Lynn loves to bake and she brought me cakes and biscuits. Tab is really creative and she brought me bunting, which she asked me to help her put together (which – as I detail later – helped me to develop fine motor skills). Yumi does energy healing and massage. Sal's good with numbers and spreadsheets and helped me with managing my supplements when I first started on my naturopathic diet. Thomas, my nephew, is good with numbers too and he helped me in the early days of this process.

I only have one friend who was into footie in a serious way. His name is John or Johnny, as he prefers to be called now. I know him from school but we only became friends years later when he was living in London and used to come round to give Tab and me massages when he was in training as a sports masseur. I thought I was supposed to ask him about football but when he next came in it was clear that this wasn't what he was "for" and instead I realised I needed to ask him to order me a "squatty potty" to help me go to the loo. I was constipated at the time and I knew he had this stool you put your feet on when on the toilet to simulate the squat position – a much more natural position for humans and one we adopted for millennia before the pedestal was introduced in 1896 (Lambert, n.d.). He duly did so but one of the physios confiscated it as it might be left in the bathroom and be a danger to less stable patients.

"What can you teach me?" became my constant, unspoken question to my friends and anyone who came my way. I thought I could come out of this stronger and better than when I went in and could pick up skills from anyone and everyone. When I was learning to walk I would walk behind people who sashayed their hips when they walked as I've always been a bit stiff and haven't used my hips in walking. I thought I could pick up a new way of walking along with new ways of doing everything I wanted to improve. My healing brain could support it and could help me change. Later, at the BIRT, my clinical psychologist, David Ruthenberg, to whom I mentioned this, questioned me about why I felt I *needed* to change. I didn't have an answer, apart from that I had always felt inadequate and not good enough.

At Schumacher College we had studied basic quantum physics. We had learned about the double-slit experiment, which proved that when something is watched it changes (Double-slit experiment, n.d.). This was brought to mind for me countless times in hospital as patients were watched the whole time. When I went to the bathroom a nurse would be with me or standing outside the open door; when I ate someone would record what I ate; when I started to walk I would always have someone beside me or just behind me. But it was more psychological than that. I would feel somehow pressured to act like I was mentally unstable in the hospital but not when I was at home or at regular Pilates or yoga classes, for instance.

Now, I'm not saying that I wasn't cognitively unstable – of course I was, I had a brain injury – but I am saying that I could get away with it in "normal" society. And it was so important to feel normal. When one of the OTs took me on a day trip to Cambridge, I felt similarly watched over and did things I never would have done, such as get embarrassed when I was at the till in a shop. It was like being taken out for the first time by a parent who wants you to order and be the grown-up and yet is still watching over you. When I made some "mistakes", such as not checking the bus time-tables before we left (because I would typically just turn up to the bus stop and check there or check Google Maps in advance) they were reported. I was always being watched over. I had to wait for the traffic lights to turn green, even if there was nothing coming to the extent that I still find myself doing it!

On that visit to Cambridge I failed to buy a return ticket on the bus, asking only for a single. Ordinarily, I would have "winged it", i.e. acted spontaneously – I didn't know whether we were going to get the bus back and we could easily have taken a taxi – but when the OT pointed it out, I felt lacking and humiliated. She didn't mean to make me feel that way at all though.

Equally, when I went to the swimming pool with Mike on one of my weekends at home I was totally free to swim and play. I had been in the pool for some time when he went off to the steam room at the side of the pool. He told me he was going there and then, just as he walked away, I saw him say something to the pool guard and gesture in my direction. I immediately felt inhibited whereas before I had felt completely free. Of course, Mike was just doing what he thought was right and I probably would have done the same but it wasn't the same for me after that. The lifeguard was watching over me like I was some kind of learner swimmer.

Disinhibition

Another result of a brain injury is disinhibition, which I used to call my filter-free stage. I called my sister fat, called a nurse with fake tan "orange", asked another if she was really going to get married with "those braces" (on her teeth) and all sorts of other insults which quite upset me when I later thought about them. It was as if I couldn't stop myself saying something that popped into my mind, which made me realise how much we all inhibit ourselves in normal life. In other cultures it isn't done to the same extent, as I realised when I was living in Malaysia and was told by a colleague one morning that I had a spot on my face. I downplayed it and the response was, "No, but it's HUGE!" Children don't have this inhibition naturally either and we need to teach them to be polite. My friend Malcolm remembers being on a bus and calling a quite young woman "little old lady", and my nieces and nephews, while they were still young, used to say the most outrageous things. They were mostly true observations though!

I think I still have some of that disinhibition remaining now but it's certainly much less extreme than it used to be.

The one about the escape

Escape was a big theme for a while, especially while I was on the Lewin Unit. I honestly thought people were trying to encourage me to escape, from nurses saying, "Oh, the doors are open again", to porters and cleaners and even friends and family (before I could walk) making exaggerated walking movements.

Before this, when I was on the A ward, Mike and my friend Malc took me outside in my wheelchair, outside the main entrance to the hospital (we hadn't yet discovered the Jubilee Gardens). I saw a man in his pyjamas and he smiled at me as he was walking away from the hospital. My thought was that he'd escaped. So it *was* possible. These thoughts were all in silence as I couldn't yet speak. Only much later did I realise he worked at Addenbrooke's and his "pyjamas" were really his scrubs.

But the scariest example was one night shift when an Italian nurse said (or I thought I heard him say), "They think my name is [O] but it's really [something like] Juan Carlos" and then laughing maniacally. He was talking about a patient who'd made a map of the hospital and was planning to escape one night when all was quiet. He was talking so loudly by my bed that I thought he was trying to communicate that if I had any kind of spirit at all I would escape. I called him to my bed and asked him if the ones I loved would be saved if I did escape as I believed then that they were all destined to end up in hospital, particularly my dad and my partner. He obviously didn't understand what I was saying and probably put it down to the delirious ramblings of a brain patient. But I honestly thought that night of escaping – I just didn't have the guts.

There was another time when I was in the dining room with another patient from my bay and she started talking about the bus stop just up the road and how cheap and easy it was to get into town. She was obviously delirious herself but I didn't realise it at the time and thought she had a message that she was trying to get across to me. There was only one staff member on duty that day in the dining room and when he put the radio on I thought he was also trying to communicate a message to me. It was a Sunday and he was talking about how quiet Sundays always were – and the songs he was playing all seemed relevant to an escape on a Sunday. "Tell me why I don't like Mondays", "My Little Runaway"....

The one about vivisection

One day I heard visitors at my neighbour's bed – they closed the curtains so I could only hear them but it was obviously the patient's grandson visiting. He was reading a book and pointing out what he saw, as children do. He must have been aged about six. He was saying, "Daddy!" and his mother was correcting him, "hedgehog". When his father appeared and walked past my bed it was amazing how much he looked like a hedgehog. For this and other reasons I thought all people were animals. Of course, we're all animals in a very real sense, all having evolved from the same source.

There was a patient on the Lewin who couldn't speak but who wrote down, "[some kind of drug/procedure] took my voice away". I thought he'd been a monkey and had been the subject of some awful experiment to be made into a human but who they couldn't train to speak. I thought I was being asked to choose between human and animal and there would be terrible consequences if I chose the wrong one. He kept motioning for me to come outside with him so that we could talk in private – as I thought – or to read something on the computer in the dining room that he was looking at, but I never went or read it. It was too early for me to face computer screens anyway. I thought I was a real coward in those days, always choosing the easy option, saving myself instead of others despite my high principles.

There was another patient who used to have a toy, a stuffed monkey, on her at all times. She had been given it by a grandchild who had a toy monkey she called Nidge – short for Nigel. One night I heard her cry out from an adjoining ward, "Nidge! They've taken Nidge!" and my neighbour in the bed next to me took up the cry, probably disturbed by the noise. She couldn't talk in any meaningful way, while I could by this time. This was enough to continue a story in my mind about monkeys being experimented on and saved by anti-vivisectionists. They had managed to break into the laboratory and steal Nidge – who had become in my mind a real monkey. It seemed to me that if I didn't speak out, monkeys and other animals would continue to be tortured and no one would speak for me when it came to my turn to be experimented on. So I rang my buzzer to let a nurse know. When he came – and I can't now remember who it was – I said, "A monkey's been taken!" – but sort of knew it wouldn't be believed, so acted as if I was dreaming. What were they going to do, phone around all the laboratories – and all on a disturbed patient's say so – to see if any monkeys had been taken and then what? Call the police? They'd probably just return the monkey to the laboratory anyway as the lab wasn't doing anything illegal. Anyway, for a number of reasons I was embarrassed – and happy to allow the nurse to think it was just the midnight ramblings of a disturbed patient. I had done my duty and that was as far as I could go, I justified it to myself. But I felt ashamed, as if I'd let a whole community down.

As I was lying in my bed in the shared bay one lunchtime (I hadn't yet made it to the dining room as I was still on feed or NG tube), I heard one nurse or HCA say to another, "Oh, such and such a nurse is so good at getting all the patients out!" and the other agreeing. I thought they were talking about getting beds back for new patients and so listened carefully, thinking there was another conspiracy at play. I had no idea they were just talking about meal times as some patients would decline to go to the dining room and have to be brought meals at their beds. I could see from my bay across to another bay and noticed a nurse – whom I will call N – in the room. I thought it must be him they were talking about being so good at getting all the patients out. As I watched I noticed N talking to a patient who I would later share a bay with. He was being so gentle with her, talking to her calmly and kindly, trying to persuade her to get up but she was determined to stay in bed. Then I noticed she had my blanket! I had not liked the blanket anyway – it was one someone had given me and it was itchy and too hot – but it was mine! I made up my mind to watch this one, she was obviously a thief! Now, looking back, she obviously didn't steal my blanket – my sister had probably told the nurses I didn't want it and it had been given to this other patient, either that or they had thought it was hers all along. Things were always moving about from table to table, going missing or just getting lost. It amazes me even now that patients' tables can be moved around so much without their doing it – cleaners come in, nurses move things around and then on the next shift other nurses assume they're someone else's. It happens.

One day after a Felipa movement session (I talk about these later) in the dining room, a patient sat in her wheelchair along from me and gave me such a stare of recognition, seeming to say with her eyes, "Don't you recognise me?" that I felt like I must know her. She did look like a younger version of my neighbour, a patient in my bay, so I believed she was a (later or earlier) version of the same person. I was also in a wheelchair at the time and I couldn't then talk. She said to me something like, "I know you and you know me and I'll be here for you until the very end". I believed her and felt safe and we formed quite a bond for several weeks until she told me she'd been mistaken, that I just had the same colour hair as her daughter-in-law. I felt abandoned and that she was denying me just as Judas had denied Jesus in the Garden of Gethsemane.

This was compounded by seeing people who looked the same or very similar – like versions of one another – all around the hospital and even in magazines – you know the ones with adverts for firms of estate agents and the like, where they put each of the team members' photos? They *all* looked like each other as if they were part of the same family – different generations of them, male and female. Even more oddly, when I was wheeled around the hospital when I was well enough to sit in the concourse – as the main public area of Addenbrooke's was known – and have a coffee or lunch, it seemed as if people were staring at me in recognition and would be giving me secret smiles and nods. Now, looking back, I realise that it was perhaps because *I* was staring at *them* but at the time it seemed the other way around. And visitors, not just mine, and people on the concourse, appeared to get tears in their eyes looking at me – that was probably true as I was so thin and feeble looking.

I also thought I saw a different version – an Indian version – of Stephan Harding, our tutor at Schumacher College. He was walking down the corridor towards me as I was being wheeled onto the hospital concourse where all the cafes were. He half smiled at me so I was sure it was him! This may have been influenced by the fact that Stephan loved India and was always doing impressions of Indian people.

I believed I was on a one-woman mission to help people remember and get back to their old selves and – probably influenced by the narrator of my yoga nidra recording – thought one older Indian patient was a Swami, a teacher. I would call him Swami-ji, a respectful address to a Swami, to help him remember who he was.

When we were all watching TV in the dining room one day – this TV set appeared later in my stay and I hated it but again was drawn to it – a "version" of one of the other patients at the table, whom I had only just met, appeared on the programme. It was him! So I called him by his "real" name, the name of the guy on the TV, with a knowing look and he pretended not to know what I was talking about! I thought I knew why he was pretending not to understand as this guy on the TV was some kind of terrorist – but he was genuinely perplexed as he corrected me on his name.

Other stories

Here are some stories that I've written up as short stories, already recognising them as fictional. It was life as seen through my psychosis but I present them here as examples of how I perceived the world and my fellow patients at the time. Now I recognise that many of these things never happened, but it's an interesting feature of psychosis that you hear and see things that absolutely never existed.

I now also know that I misheard certain other things like nurses talking about "getting a fix" at Costa and thinking they were talking about drugs when they were only talking about caffeine!

The energy vampire

Paul walks into the room – no, that's not quite right, *wheels* into the room – takes a look around and settles for a place next to the newcomer. He needs an energy boost and this one will do. Flatter him first:

"I've been watching you and I'm intrigued. Tell me, how do you know so much about people from just a few minutes of talking to them?"

The newcomer looks surprised. "Do I? I didn't know that I did that."

"Of course you know. I really admire people who have such strong intuition. It's something I can't do with ease." He wants it for himself and he's going to get it.

Paul sits back while someone brings him his lunch. The newcomer is hooked. But Paul's an expert at this. He won't give anything more away until he's asked for it.

The newcomer just stares fixedly at Paul. Pleading with his eyes. Nothing much happens around here and Paul is the most interesting person he's met all day (all week if truth be told). Yes, he has an inkling that Paul is dangerous but in a "bad boy" kind of way, and this week he wants to be in with the bad boys.

"I'm sure you can. But give me an example. How do I act on my intuition?"

It's just the prompt Paul needs to continue.

"Like the other day, when you told that nurse to fuck off."

"I never did that!"

"Not in words, you didn't. But your body language told him in no uncertain terms. The way you refused his care when he tried to feed you. I've had a bad feeling about him too but didn't have the confidence to act on it."

Over the next few days Paul sunk his teeth into his most recent victim and he, in turn, became weaker and weaker, talking less and turning up to meals less often. Paul started to recover, even began to attend the weekly movement class and to get dressed for meals sometimes. Eventually this other man was released and I never saw him again.

You had to admire Paul for his chutzpah, but at the same time I disliked him, was afraid of him even. He followed me out once into the garden, told me he couldn't follow me onto the grass as I could walk and he was in a wheelchair, and that he liked me, making me feel guilty but stalked at the same time.

Bacteria

I remember ...

Looking across at the patient opposite, and seeing her reading something behind my bed, scanning and then, as I looked at her, pretending not to. What was she looking at? Of course! Her bacteria were learning the language of humans.

"Please turn me."

"No thank you, I won't have any antibiotics."

"May I have a lollipop, please?"

They're so much more sophisticated than their hosts. They were here first, creating life from chemical vents under the ocean. They specialise in horizontal gene transfer. They've hitched lifts to the moon. They live off and with hosts so numerous and diverse that their survival is guaranteed. Being able to morph into any form, travelling on clouds. Being able to withstand radioactivity far greater than anything found on Earth. (And why is that? They must have grand plans!)

And now learning the language of their human hosts and so being able to say no to killer antibiotics, yes to sugar: a rare feat indeed.

Breathe in and hold

Breathe in and hold. The bacteria will suffocate and die, killing their human host of course, but that's not my problem. Anyway, Fat Freddy has to die. Generation after generation of him, with different bacteria in charge but always Fat Freddy.

He was there in the dining room the other day, watching me. I couldn't turn around as I was in a wheelchair but I felt him and saw him out of the corner of my eye. He didn't like me being there one little bit. He could tell I was part of the new generation, the one that would leapfrog over his, be able to eat, not be confined to a wheelchair. And he didn't want to be surpassed. He was jealous of what I would inevitably become. I would one day walk out of this place whereas he would be stuck here forever. He was talking to his people, telling them to get rid of me and I was scared. He had people working for him in here and I couldn't be sure which nurses were in on it. I couldn't be too careful. Who I spoke to, what I ate, it was all important. They were trying to keep me in here but I would get out eventually!

Drugs

Henry was a drugs dealer. Where was the best place to score drugs? A hospital, of course. So when he had a stroke and ended up in one he was overjoyed. Nurses working long shifts were both his clients and his suppliers/accomplices. He would get them to prescribe drugs that he wouldn't take but would then sell back to them.

They operated at night, after the staff nurse had gone home.

"Who's the boss?" the cry would go out.

"I'm the boss now!" one of them would announce. I knew it was code for "open house on drugs".

The nurses and HCAs were always losing the keys to the mobile drugs cabinets. "Can I borrow your keys?" was a familiar question around the wards.

Sometimes nurses would plant drugs on patients or store them in their bedside lockers – the lock-ups – to which only they had the keys.

I remember waking up one night to see one of the nurses leaving drugs and syringes on my bed. "I'm going to be implicated," I thought with horror.

And another night overhearing a group of staff, mostly nurses, talking about where they went to get a fix – apparently Costa was open 24 hours a day. The perfect place to get high.

I was shocked how open some of them were about it. Lying in the corridor one day, waiting to be moved from one bay to another, I heard one of the cleaners visit the bathroom. He gave a shout, somewhere between pain and pleasure. It was obvious he was shooting up. Easy access to needles? Tick. To drugs? Tick. To customers? Tick, tick, tick.

Another time I came back from the dining room to see one young nurse's nose rimmed with white powder – didn't she know it was visible? Hadn't someone told her? I stared at it, making sure it was obvious, but she didn't bat an eyelid.

Henry was also a seer. Or pretended to be. At nights he would call name after name, supposedly at random, but in fact they were all the names of nurses and HCAs. One by one they would all be called to his bedside, some going willingly, others more reluctantly.

Henry was very weak one night and sleeping in a side room and I heard a group of nurses conferring outside his room. Some of them seemed to owe him money, others wanted a fix. They agreed that they would murder him in his bed.[2]

There was a brief struggle and I could just make out Henry saying, "No! Not the pillow!" and then it was over. It seemed amazing to me that they would do it in plain sight of – or at least within the hearing of – other patients.

Nein, nein, nein! (Nancy's story)

Nancy shouted out at night. She was there before me, slightly mad as most of us were. I heard her on my first night.

"Notice her! Please notice her!" she would shout. I would think, "Who?" but she didn't elaborate so I just thought she meant another patient. Possibly one with a full catheter bag. I thought she was trying to do some good.

"Nein, nein, nein!" This was getting more interesting. Perhaps Nancy had spent time in Germany or at least was familiar with the language. My partner's grandparents had escaped Hitler in the war and it was a typical story.

Then it turned into "Notice here. Police notice here" and "999", as if she were trying to call the police for help or had noticed a police notice by the side of the road in her memory.

I thought of the quote or poem by Martin Niemöller, which I had heard so many times I knew it by heart:

> First they came for the socialists, and I did not speak out – because I was not a socialist.
> Then they came for the trade unionists, and I did not speak out – because I was not a trade unionist.
> Then they came for the Jews, and I did not speak out – because I was not a Jew.
> Then they came for me – and there was no one left to speak for me.

Of course! Nancy was German! It all fit together beautifully now! She was German and had been complicit through silence with the Nazis – their raids on all her neighbours, and now she was all alone!

The power of speech

I could vocalise long before I could speak out loud. I believed I was part of a group similar to the group in the 1990 film *Awakenings* where Robin Williams "awakens" a group of catatonic patients with the help of a drug. (This film was based on the book *Awakenings* by Oliver Sacks (1973) in which a group of patients with Encephalitis Lethargica (sleeping-sickness) were for a time awoken when given the drug L-Dopa.)

Nurses would always be trying to elicit a thumbs-up sign from me, which I didn't understand the reason for at the time. I now know that it was to establish a form of communication so that I could indicate yes (thumbs up) and no (thumbs down). Then it progressed to a paper onto which were written the words, YES and NO, which I was meant to indicate.

Sometimes I would know what I wanted the answer to be and indicate or circle it and then my hand would automatically travel to the opposite answer and indicate or circle that. It was as if I had no physical control over it. Sometimes "my" answer was not represented by these binary options and would consist of something subtler like "I don't know", or "sort of", or "let's try it and see" to a question like "Would you like your bed raised?" But at this stage I couldn't write, to add more options.

Going back to the *Awakenings* story, in my mind I'd witnessed other patients' "awakenings" and was doing research on the best way to help people like me. So every day I would confide my latest "findings" to Mike in a whisper. He thought this hilarious and went along with it, to the extent that I thought he was "in on it", whatever "it" was. I thought *he* was spying on *me*, and reporting back to the hospital authorities! I also thought we were all Jewish (Mike is) and that's why I was on the Lewin Unit (a typically Jewish name) and that his grandfather – who had now sadly passed away – was profiting from it all. I thought if I could persuade his grandfather to make a large donation I would be able to get out of hospital. I thought I had married my father (Mike and my dad's face looked very similar to me at the time, especially bending down over me) and that all my friends were Jewish too. One good friend in particular, Sal, on her first visit, seemed to have her nose growing and shrinking, telling me that not only was she Jewish (?!), her body was being taken over by successive generations of bacteria, i.e. new versions of bots.

I thought there were multiple generations of the same family on the Lewin, including mine, and whenever I heard a name that was one of my family members that it actually was them, even if they had been dead for years. I thought we were all animals and that vivisection was going on and the animals were getting their own back on us. I thought countless things and have written these up as short stories, some of which I've included above. But one of the strongest themes was that of drug trials, which I'll go into here as it's an example of the power of the brain to distort reality.

Drug trials

Each patient with a wheelchair had their cushion type printed on a piece of paper and tied or stuck to the back of their wheelchair. This meant that you could never see your own when sitting in it. I thought it referred to the drug trial you were on. For example, I caught sight of mine one day as it was backed up to my bed and it read "BLUE GEL DYNAMITE". I thought this must be the name of a drug. The fact that my nickname is Jel (Gel) only seemed to confirm it. From my reading about the brain it seems that there's a certain state – a hypnotic dream state – which Van Der Kolk (2015) calls a hypnagogic or trance state – where things connect without the logic of everyday thinking:

> Trance states, during which theta activity dominates, can help to loosen the conditioned connections between particular stimuli and responses … some patients report unusual imagery and/or deep insights about their life.

And:

> When theta waves predominate in the brain, the mind's focus is on the internal world, a world of free-floating imagery.

But so many things seemed to corroborate it. I overheard the nurses at mealtimes talking about the patients "on trials" and seeming to include me in that group. I overheard a doctor on the first ward I was in once say that the injection that I was given every night, a warfarin equivalent, was "devil's juice". I overheard the doctors in my bay on their day rounds discussing other patients and whether they needed to be on these drugs. Whether any of these things actually happened I don't know, but they were true for me.

I found on my bedside table one day a pump bottle labelled "Double-base Gel" which, as it turned out, my father had left for me and is simply a mainstream emollient, but I thought it meant that I was to learn the double bass (double bass Jel)!

I was all potential in those days – like a stem cell, like a baby.

Another story that was very strong for me was that of robots or "bots" as I called them. I thought we were all bots, that the staff including the cleaner were bots, and that I was one of the later generations. There were nursebots, cleanerbots, patientbots, all sorts of bots. I even asked one of the nurses (in writing as I couldn't yet speak) if she was a "bot" (Figure 5.3).

I remember my friend Sally coming to visit me. She's a mother to two children and I helped her out sometimes when her eldest, Bella, was a baby.

She knew I needed to sleep and I knew she knew the rule "no eye contact" with babies when you're putting them to bed as she'd told me about it many times. So I kept looking at her and smiling whenever she looked back. I was just being cheeky the way I normally would but it was this that told her I was "in there".

I thought that she was a robot (bot) and could teach me the latest language. I even wrote it down: "Teach me your latest language." She didn't know what I was talking about but she questioned me with such a twinkle in her eye that I didn't believe her. I thought that she thought it just wasn't time for that yet, that I wasn't ready for it.

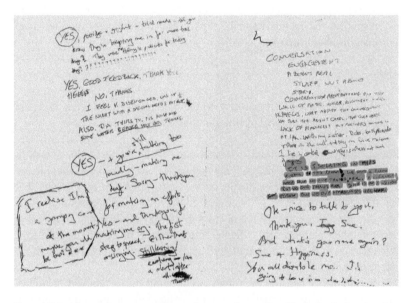

Figure 5.3 Note about excellent cleaner. It reads: "It is isolating in this room. In this room. We have a clean area but no one thanks her. A cleaner but no one thanks her. She is an excellent person but no one appreciates her work."

There was obviously a language that we "bots" could communicate with so as not to arouse suspicion. And it wasn't voiced. The first models were still on the binary – yes and no; the second generation had developed a "maybe" and the third a totally different language, maybe not even verbal, a series of signs perhaps, or something even subtler, like hand squeezes. My own mother seemed to know this language – she would always squeeze my hand several times on greeting me. I thought she was trying to teach me the new language but that I was too stupid to learn it. I thought that if I spoke in verbal language this would make me unable to learn the new language of bots.

Choices: deaf or hearing?

When people first started trying to get me to speak, especially the Speech and Language Therapy team, or SALT as they're known, I thought they were trying to make me deaf as they seemed to be talking so loudly. I even thought they looked deaf themselves. This became another story: I was being asked to choose between the deaf and hearing world, especially when I was allowed onto the concourse and noticed a hearing loop in Marks & Spencer. All the nurses seemed to have a hearing loop sign on their phones, all websites I looked at seemed to have hearing/deaf options and so on. I eventually chose hearing and again felt like a deserter, a coward.

This was similar to being asked to choose between a male and female brain as I believed I remembered earlier.

The Speech and Language Therapy (SALT) team interviewed me one day using a form that I assumed was designed to catch me out. I thought my family had filled it in and the therapist was testing my memory to see if it had been affected. In fact, she was just trying to get me to speak. Of course, I knew all the answers – it was all about me, for goodness' sake! – but at the time I was trying not to let on that I could speak and I thought the best way to do this was to pretend I was mentally disturbed. So I fudged the answers and pretended I couldn't remember and acted as if I really was "special needs". I didn't like it when doctors and nurses assumed I was "not all there" though and talked down to me, as I saw it. I was terribly sensitive to being patronised.

I was always being asked to devise my own strategies, it seemed. But, I thought, I'd never been in this situation before! Surely the professionals should know what works? This is probably why I believed I was always being tested. I now know that no one strategy works for everyone and that if they had tried to impose strategies on me it would have become frustrating and hindered my development.

An example of this is when a speech and language therapist had discovered – through my sister, Debs – that childhood songs were helping me to vocalise as I would complete them when they were sung. Being unfamiliar with these songs the SALT suggested we look them up on the internet. I had thought it a good idea at the time, but when we sat in front of the computer I knew it wasn't. Screens were too much for me in those days – too much stimulation of all kinds: light, pictures, movement, sound, everything together. I couldn't work the keyboard at all, I was shaking so much. And worse, I started pulling at my hair and in my memory of it, it started coming out in my hands, huge clumps of it. I had already told the SALT I thought I was going mad with all these crazy patients, lack of sleep and all the rest of it.

I cried, "I really *am* going mad. Look, I'm pulling out my own hair!" It must have been that the hair had been weakened by the operation and the SALT writes in her report that I was mistaken in thinking it was huge clumps of hair. But that's how it seemed to me at the time.

On the first day that the SALT missed one of our appointments (therapists used to write their slots on the timetable at the end of patients' bed, weekly) I again thought it was a test – this time of how much I wanted to recover and get out of the Lewin. So I spoke to her colleague who'd kindly come to break the news and broke down in tears – partly because I was genuinely upset but partly also to demonstrate how much I wanted the session. I knew she'd report it back to the SALT and the team.

Choices: human or animal?

Yet another choice was between a human and an animal. I saw a patient who looked like a monkey (in my eyes) and thought he'd just come out of the lab, now transformed into human shape. He couldn't talk and wrote that it was because of a drug or operation: "Can't speak due to [name of a drug or procedure]." That confirmed my suspicions about drug trials. It was all interwoven.

Voices from my subconscious

I used to write things and draw on my pad of file paper before I could talk, and often I felt the pen was being guided so that things would just appear. There was one time, early on in the Lewin, when I was moved to a side room because a patient on the ward I'd been on (the A ward) had developed MRSA and they moved me as a precaution. Suddenly, MRSA started to appear in my doodlings and I was convinced I had it, to the extent that Mike asked the staff nurse to write a declaration that I didn't have MRSA.

I started drawing Vs in the same way as the Vegan Society logo (like a tick), which convinced me that I should become vegan. I must have driven the staff half mad with my vegetarian/vegan declarations, not to mention my poor sister, who brought in meals for me only to be told of my new dietary preferences, which changed almost every day. I also had a thing about not eating sugar and would almost always refuse a dessert, but I now know that this was the right instinct.

Also oxygen seemed a theme, whether noticing signs for oxygen on patients' beds or a member of the staff team talking about a boxing event he was taking part in at the O2 in London. I'm now having hyperbaric oxygen therapy to bring oxygen into my cells, important for fighting cancer as well as many cell functions.

I now think – no, I know – that these doodles and observation were all things I'd read or seen, but not consciously. For example, when I was out of bed one time I looked above my bed to see the name of my clinician – and saw "Dr Kilmore". Not only was I now even more convinced that Mr Helmy had not operated on me, but I read Dr Kirker's name as Kilmore (Kill More). Dr Kirker is the head of the Lewin Unit. It was only many months later when I went to see my homeopath that I saw that the house next door was called Kilmore. I hadn't consciously noticed this before, but it had obviously lodged in my subconscious and come back to me ominously.

I suppose this is why advertising agencies say that you only have to see things three times to believe them and why advertising can be so damaging, particularly advertising for junk food and fashion during children's programmes.

I found myself drawing a figure eight time after time, sometimes on its side like this (Figure 5.4), which is the sign for infinity.

I read it to mean that I was destined for immortality, which I'm sure fed many of my internal stories. It must have been excruciatingly annoying to the other patients, but I used to draw this symbol over and over on the dining table with plastic cups, making a horrible noise! I remember one patient just holding up a finger to stop me, which worked. It was a big relief – not just for the other patients! And when I saw a patient with a necklace bearing an infinity sign on a chain, I thought she was really special and had been sent with a message for me. I thought she was somehow related to me even. I used to think I wanted a tattoo of a leminscate going up my spine and that this would somehow protect me and make me immortal. I still think about it, sometimes, though I no longer want to be immortal.

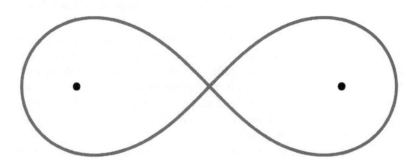

Figure 5.4 Infinity sign.

One of the nutritionists used to sing or hum "Karma Chameleon" by Culture Club every time she walked onto my bay. I now realise that – consciously or subconsciously – she had seen the wire chameleon that a friend had brought me back from South Africa and which I had hung above my bed.

Another example of my subconscious interfering with my conscious is when I started to use the word "excellent" about everybody, an unusual word for me to use of people. And "kind" and "trust" and "safe" as in "I trust you", "You're excellent", "You're so kind" or "I feel safe with you". It was particularly apt that I used to apply these epithets to a nurse called Nessie so that they became Kindnessie (kindness) or Excellentnessie (excellentness)!

I couldn't yet read the hospital values sheet as the print was so small and my eyes were still adjusting, yet these were the hospital values, stuck up on sheets in every bay.

Addenbrooke's Trust Values

Safe: I never walk past, I always speak up.

Kind: I always take care of the people around me.

Excellent: I'm always looking for a better way.

When later I was doing affirmations to try to influence my healing, I would take down this sheet in the side room as I believed it was trying to undermine my affirmations. The detail (for example, "I never walk past, I always speak up") was written in tiny type that I couldn't read from my bed, so I thought it was trying to give me subliminal messages.

Insights into my own personality

I thought I overheard things which couldn't possibly have been said – they were part of my psychosis. I overheard one day two nurses discussing me and saying, "That one doesn't like to put other people out – she just won't ask for help", which I've realised since is absolutely true of me, and which I'm working on. It's an interesting facet of psychosis that one's subconscious or spirit self comes in and delivers messages to one's conscious self. In fact, in many other cultures what is here labelled psychosis or mental illness is heralded as a gift to the community, to be nurtured and guided.

I also heard myself being labelled as a "social type", which I remember as a category from a piece of fundraising consulting work I did years ago for RNIB (Royal National Institute of Blind People). The RNIB had brought in an agency to classify their donor database into groups so that they could more accurately target their fundraising messages. For example, donors were grouped into social types – "I just want the world to be a better place"; enlightened self-interest – "I'm so lucky not to have sight issues/there but for the grace of God ..."; and by which newspapers they read and so on.

Though the nurses couldn't possibly have known that I use a brand of phone called a Fairphone – I certainly wasn't ready to use it back then so didn't have it with me and hardly anyone's ever heard of a Fairphone – I heard them talking about me. They were saying, "Oh, she's likely to read the *Guardian* or the *Independent*, use a Fairphone, bank with the Co-operative Bank or Triodos ...." All of which I do. But I thought, "Oh, they've researched and really know me!" They went on to say that I would probably want to help other patients, which I did and got into trouble for too with some members of staff as some nurses thought I was overstepping my role as patient.

I read over my notes from the time and I've written:

> I cannot help any of them, just as no one will be able to help me, should that be my future! And the nurses won't listen anyway.
> "Doesn't matter," says Javier [an Ayuhuasca shaman who Mike and I met in Peru].

Later, I read in the notes above the bed of the patient opposite me the words "Believes she is saved", which I took to mean that she was religious.

But there were never notes like these, only notes that referred to eating and how to treat that particular patient, such as "Liz likes Radio 4" or "Soft diet only" or "Allow plenty of time for Alex to respond".

I now realise that this "Believes she is saved" was about me and my egotistic assumptions that I, above all the rest of the patients, was special in some way and had saviours all around. But this was probably a large part of the reason that I made such progress, so it wasn't all bad.

There was a computer on a stand at eye height that the nurses used to wheel around with the drugs trolley. On the stand was written "Just Stand", which must have been the name of the brand of the equipment but which I read as a message for me before I could walk, "Just stand! Just get up and do it!" More so when nurses would park it – to me it seemed very slowly and deliberately – in front of my bed.

The infamous falls alarm sounded like "false alarm" and "Tab's Voice", which was written on the alarm bell, as if my friend Tab were speaking for me. And the Tork brand of hygiene products always seemed to be a message to "talk".

I later saw many people in Brain Tumour Charity or Trust t-shirts, out for a run or walk in public and made up my mind that once I was well, I would do a sponsored activity for one of these charities.

Hypnosis

I thought the nurses were all trying to hypnotise the patients as I would frequently hear them say things under their breath as they passed my bed. I heard "child's pose" (the name of a yoga *asana* or posture) a number of times as I was doing yoga in bed and I would feel forced to obey. Once, at night, I heard a nurse say "Reiki" under his breath to me as I lay there thinking about my UTI (urinary tract infection). It seemed like a message to me that this was my route both to healing myself and to getting out of hospital. If I could heal enough people perhaps they'd let me out. I made a promise there and then that I would go round giving Reiki healing to anyone who needed it, but it wasn't to be. I was a patient. The closest I got to it was giving massages one meal time and giving Reiki healing to one or two patients.

I did offer a massage to one nurse after a night shift but he said he was okay. He must have thought me very odd! He was a bank nurse, meaning that he wasn't full time but a sort of locum nurse employed from a "bank" of nurses[3] – he was surprised that I remembered his name the next time he was working but of course I had. I had been watching him all night, being so nice to the "special" patient on my bay. She shared a name with a good friend from my Master's course at Schumacher College (I'll call her C) so naturally I believed it was another version of her and I felt particularly fond of her. I tried to comfort C one night when she was up and down and trying to get out of her bed. The nurses wanted me to go back to my own bed but I emptied my catheter bag all over the floor to distract them! I sat with C and she told me to go back to my own bed too, muttering something about my husband and my own protection, obviously under some illusion, as many of us were.

But as I watched that night, unable to sleep with the fascination of trying to understand what C was up to, she acted out some scenes – or I thought she did – of women working as opposed to not working. It was like a play where my mind filled in the narration and put things together. She and this nurse were acting in the play together, it seemed to me. There was another nurse who was getting fed up with C's behaviour or pretending to be, with C making a mess everywhere and never cleaning it up. C was rich and spoilt in one version and her husband was evil, taking everything from her once she was in hospital, a reflection of how I thought Mike was behaving towards me at the time I now suppose. I also remember witnessing a neighbour, another patient, losing her wallet and diary and me thinking it had been stolen, maybe by a nurse, maybe by her nephew who would come and visit her, stay in her house, sort out her financial affairs and always with such a well-meaning air. And what, I thought at the time, is *that* concealing?! As I said I was deeply suspicious of everyone and everything. Then C was miming working at a supermarket checkout, getting fitter as she got more independent. The message I got very clearly was *women should work to maintain their physical health and independence*. I made sure that I made my own bed the next morning and did it most mornings after that.

Seeing things

My friend Bron went to South Africa on holiday shortly after my operation and sent daily videos to keep in touch. I couldn't at first focus on the screen but when I could, with Mike holding the phone so that I could see it, it appeared as though she was in a wheelchair in the videos. I watched them on Mike's iPhone and thought the picture quality was odd, but assumed they were in a new version to my own phone. It wasn't obvious at first that she was in a wheelchair but the more I watched, the more obvious it became. Everything was being shot from a seated position, I could actually see the wheels in one shot and so on. It was as if she were saying to me, "You see, even I'm in a wheelchair – and now I can let you in on my secret. It's okay if you're going to be in a wheelchair – you're not alone." When I told her later she thought it was a rather scary prophecy, but it was comforting to me at the time.

Another friend had left me her iPad with two films loaded onto it so that I could watch them when I was alone and bored. She clearly overestimated my capacity to watch a screen. But when I did try to watch one, *8 Women*, it looked like the main character, who was in a wheelchair, got out of it at one point. I knew it couldn't be real as it was my second time of watching and this hadn't happened before. But how do you not trust your eyes when something like that happens? And the granddaughter grew in size as I watched, then shrank again, which also hadn't happened the first time around.

Other films were different too – I remember watching the other film she had left, which was Prokofiev's *Peter and the Wolf* (a short animation set to the original music with no words), with Mike and having a completely different viewing of the film to him, with completely different scenes. I've just watched it again now, and seen it as he must have seen it.

There's one scene where the moon is full and I remember it as being a smiley (acid) face, which it isn't at all! This led on to drugs scenes in the film, which are not there on watching it again. I was obviously subconsciously thinking of my own past when I played occasionally with recreational drugs like ecstasy and was afraid it was all going to come back to bite me. I've just had an "aha" moment as I write this – the whole drugs theme must have related to this. And I thought there was a young female patient who'd overdosed on drugs on the A ward early on in my stay on that ward – there may or may not have been in reality.

I'd also seen part of the film before we watched it together and in one scene I saw something completely different the last time, almost as if it were a different version of the film, different scenes that the director had decided to cut. The film had stopped there as if, again, some higher power were trying to stop me from going any further.

Notes

1 I have changed the name for confidentiality reasons.
2 I now know this didn't happen and could never have happened, at least not at Addenbrooke's: it was just my psychosis that was making me believe that what I was hearing was real.
3 Of course, never having heard this term, it led to all sorts of (now) hilarious misunderstandings – were these nurses really from the banking sector?

Chapter 6

Cancer

Alex Jelly

When Mr Helmy came to my bedside about a week or two after the operation to tell me that the biopsy had revealed the tumour to be malignant (i.e. cancerous), I didn't believe him. It was partly his dispassionate delivery, I'm sure, at which my current self isn't at all surprised or disappointed – he is a surgeon after all, and must have to break this kind of news regularly. It was partly, though, that I was under the illusion that I was an "outlier" who had survived against all the odds and was getting better faster than anyone previously or currently in my position. I thought I had heard the nurses talking outside my bay about this and actually using the word "outlier".

A few years earlier I had read a book by Malcolm Gladwell (2008), *Outliers: The Story of Success*, about people who achieved things way outside the normal curve and it had apparently made quite an impression on me.

I still didn't know for sure whether the operation had actually happened or not. Not having access to a mirror and finding the photos taken on mobile phones too hard to look at, I could have had anything done. I expect that, even had I had access to a mirror or been able to focus on those photos, I would probably have believed that the "Alice band" of stitches (Figure 6.1) and all the dried blood were part of some elaborate experiment.

Maybe I was in the placebo group, being told I had a brain tumour and an operation to remove it to see how I would perform against another group who actually had both. Either that or I *had* had both and was recovering so quickly that they had to throw other things at me. At any rate, I was convinced that I was being studied, experimented on.

Similarly, when my partner wheeled me down to Oncology for my first appointment with my future neuro-oncologist and the neuro-oncology nurse practitioner, I thought the same – that it was all part of an elaborate experiment to see how I'd react. If I survived this and got them to admit it,

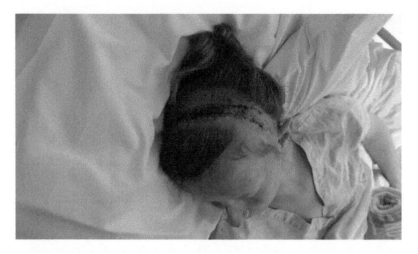

Figure 6.1   Me with an "Alice band" of stitches.

maybe they'd let me out. I was surprised, but by this time not shocked, that my partner was in on it. In fact, I tried to get him to admit it when I wailed in the waiting area afterward – with real tears – "I never thought I'd be part of the cancer club!" Another man there waiting had tears in his eyes when he heard this and a woman was openly weeping. I thought "aha!" and assumed they were actors. But Mike didn't crack.

I remember exactly when I finally realised that I had cancer. It was on a day when my older sister Cat and my friend Sally had just left.[1] At this time I had just started to use my mobile phone again, and staying in a side room to try to escape the noise on the wards I looked up this tumour on my phone to understand it better. We hadn't been using the C-word between us, any of my friends or family. Perhaps they didn't want to scare me. What I read was that the mortality rate after three years was just 50 per cent. That meant that my life was on a coin toss. As Mike already had read these stats and come to terms with them, he was unperturbed and put his usual positive spin on them. I had just found out and was shocked. I phoned my sister who was with Sally on the train home.

Cat was the best person to speak to as her son, my oldest nephew, Thomas, had had osteosarcoma when he was just 11 and had been in hospital in London, where I lived at the time, for almost a year having chemotherapy and a knee replacement. I spent a lot of time with him, cooking for him (when he would eat it) and entertaining him. It was fun and I have maintained this close bond with my first nephew. Osteosarcoma has similar odds. She told me that stats were just stats and that some people had to fall into the survivors' group. I then talked to Sally, who told me later that Cat had been a complete hero. It was reactions like these – and I had them from almost everyone I knew – that contributed to my already positive attitude. Every time I faltered there would be an angel in the form of one of my friends or family waiting to pick me up. How could I fall with all that support?

Note

1 Looking at my notes from the time, this was likely to have been on or around 19 April 2017.

Chapter 7

Rehabilitation and recovery

Alex Jelly

The A ward

The A ward was where I started my recovery, after intensive care or ICU. It was where I started moving, in part, but I was not walking when I left the A ward a few weeks after the operation.

My first (public) move

I'd moved and been moved by physios and nurses in my bed, behind closed curtains, but my hands and fingers and arms were the first parts of my body, along with my head, that I could move independently. As described earlier, I used to strengthen them at night using the bed rails and during the day by giving hand massages to others. I remember shaking hands with one doctor and him being very surprised as apparently that was the first time a patient at my stage of recovery had shaken hands with him.

Anyway, a cleaner had been cleaning around my bed for the last few days as there was a sink beside my bed for common use. He never looked at me, probably out of politeness. As he stood with his back to me, doing something at the sink, I reached out my arm to see if I could reach him. I could. So I hooked my first and second fingers into his uniform (I can't remember if it was his belt or another part of his uniform). He, of course, turned around to see what was going on and alerted one of his colleagues, who happened to be a member of the SALT team. I think I did it just because I could, but when she came to see what was going on and found my fingers in a vice-like grip around part of his uniform, I released them and made the V-sign at her – and not as a sign of peace! That was to be my signature over the next couple of weeks until Mike and my family dissuaded me from doing it. It was my way of showing a little personality and demonstrating I was "in there". I usually accompanied it with a smile to lessen its aggressive impact.

There was a woman with dementia, whom I'll call V, on the A ward with me. She filled me with horror as I realised I might someday be like her. She had a falls alarm on a cushion underneath her, as given to patients who were deemed unable to move without assistance. Nevertheless she would continually get up, and not realise the alarm's noise was produced by her movements. There was a constant cry from nurses and visitors, including Mike, of "sit down V!"

When a nurse said to a colleague that they should treat her with compassion, as his father had suffered with dementia, I liked him immediately – here was someone I could rely on for help if I ever got to that stage! There was another nurse, too, who was really kind to her, sitting with her and talking night after night. I never got to thank her for this but I'm hoping she or a colleague is reading this.

The Lewin Rehabilitation Unit

The Lewin Unit at Addenbrooke's is for stroke and neuro patients. This is where I made most of my physical recovery and started to speak. It's also where I had psychosis, which sort of protected me from the harsh reality of what was going on, though it was scary at the time.

There were several times of terror and fear in hospital, particularly in the early days when the psychosis was strong. I believed I would be there for all eternity and that no one would know. I would be there in my body but it would change – to the outside world I would die after a few weeks or months, but in reality new hosts of bacteria would come in and colonise me and I'd take on a new physical form but still be me. The "proof" of this was that Mike knew all the names of the other patients in my bay and I would fall asleep and wake up sometimes to find him by their bedsides, helping them and chatting to them. Well now, how would he know them if he wasn't part of a conspiracy to keep us all there and had been visiting for several months? He must have made a deal that he would visit us on the condition that he would always be a visitor and be able to live his own life if we would be the patients. And we would be incarcerated in here for all eternity. A ridiculous idea (although it would make a great story), but it seemed true at the time. Several other people seemed to visit different patients at the same time, which I suppose was possible.

We had a bathroom per four-bed bay and one day I was in ours and saw a big red button on the wall. I'd seen it before and wondered what it was for. It was obviously some kind of alarm, but I couldn't resist pressing it.

There was a huge noise and I realised I'd heard this noise before. It was an emergency alarm that summoned all the staff in the area to come immediately, almost regardless of what they were doing. I rushed out of the bathroom crying, "False alarm! False alarm!" (which sounded to me like "falls alarm") and when I was later admonished for it I argued that it shouldn't be within easy reach of patients. Similarly, when a nurse first left the call bell on my bed and told me to press it if I needed anything, I pressed it and pressed it almost continuously for about a minute. Various nurses came in to see what it was that I wanted and, of course, I didn't want anything, I just wanted to press the call bell. It was as if I had no control over it. I understand now that it must have been perseveration, a condition that seems to go with SMA Syndrome which makes you repeat an action over and over.

The highlight of my week on the Lewin Unit was the Friday movement session held by a dance/movement specialist, Felipa Pereira-Stubbs. Felipa had studied in the US as part of a month-long scholarship to see how they implemented dance practice in US hospitals, and to visit dance practitioners who worked with older populations. She was perfect for me as I'd already had experience of what's known as "authentic movement", in other words, letting your body move as it feels like doing, intuitively. I'd done a course in it – twice – at Schumacher College, but outside of the Master's: once in the summer before I signed up for my MSc, to try to get to know Schumacher, and again for my dissertation on "How we know the world through our bodies". And she (Felipa) was lovely.

My first session with Felipa was on a Friday early on in the Lewin. Mike had found out about it and thought I'd be interested. I was still mute and in a wheelchair but I went along with two of my friends, a couple, Katie and Mark, whom he'd arranged to be there as a surprise and whom Felipa had kindly allowed in. Usually it was patients only or so I thought until Felipa later told me that she was always open to family and friends joining in: "It's an inclusive group, and important for all people to experience how they can support the aftermath of stroke."

We later went to a Storytelling Camp in her woods just outside Cambridge on one of my weekends out of the BIRT. She was like a little piece of heaven to me, especially when I found out, through the business card that she left me, that she'd studied the effects of movement and music on stroke patients as part of a Winston Churchill Scholarship, the same scholarship as my natural building mentor, Barbara Jones, had won to explore straw-bale buildings worldwide. I thought this was a sign that we were destined to meet. We'd danced with some of the same people, read some of the same books on movement and were familiar with other people in each other's networks so we probably would have met at some point.

When Mark offered to dance with me in that first session, I felt I could get up out of my chair and move around the room with his support. It would have been the first time I stood since the operation. But the moment passed. It was just like the day I was admitted to A&E, when I felt I *could* speak if only I was given more time. Mark – and Katie – said he had two left feet. This was before I could talk but I really felt like saying (and was saying in my head), "No, he hasn't. He's just always been told that!"

Similarly, when my brother-in-law came to visit with my sister, we had a sort of sports day on the way back from the local field. It was off the road but on a path so we had plenty of flat ground to play around. My two nephews and niece were there and we played running games, Hannah taught me to skip for the first time since the operation, Josh taught me to jump across the path, and Thomas supported me to do handstands. But there was a moment when Hannah was teaching us all one of those games children play where two of you clap your hands in rhythm with a very basic tune – "A sailor went to sea, sea, sea to see what he could see, see, see …". The co-ordination is challenging until you get used to it and Andy, my brother-in-law, was saying "I'm rubbish at this" and again I was thinking but not saying, "No, no, you're not! You've just always been told that!" We can be so limited by what we hear about ourselves, especially if we're compared to others, typically siblings. "Oh, he's the linguist/musician", our parents might say about our sibling, or "She's the mathematician in the family", leading us to think that we're not.

I was so light that my youngest nephew was carrying me on his back at one point and Cat, my sister – she's so brilliant like this – was supporting me, with my legs around her waist, to do sit-ups. Her daughter, my niece Hannah, is a gymnast so Cat's used to these kinds of things. I was exhausted afterwards but happy like a child who's been playing all day and needs to sleep. I slept so well that afternoon after they had left. It was my family (especially my partner, but also my sisters and my dad) and friends who were my best physios, always challenging me and playing with me. We used to play with balls, catching and throwing, and Mike would always be the one changing direction and hands and encouraging me to do the same. Sometimes the ball would land on one of the other patients' beds if we were playing in the ward and then we would get into trouble. But I didn't care and secretly thought it was good for the other patients, though on this last point I was probably wrong.

Anyway, back to Felipa! Often Felipa's music would make one patient or other cry. Perhaps the words would remind us of something, perhaps music just has that special potential to touch the soul. I found myself crying on more than one occasion and couldn't have told you why. I just knew that I loved those sessions. I found I couldn't, though, talk and dance at the same time, and found it easier to move with my eyes half-closed. The sessions were always too short and Felipa would go off to another part of the hospital to take more patients through movement. Sometimes she would stay and chat and I found this slightly embarrassing because I, usually so articulate, was not at all at this point and I had so much I wanted to talk about with her. But she was almost certainly used to it.

Learning to walk again

The nurses and OTs were helpful in everything except learning to walk again – that was the physio team's job – but the nurses and OTs helped in ways I didn't realise at the time.

Some of the physios were particularly skilled at helping patients to regain movement. I know a couple of them were my best teachers in movement. One in particular used to pay attention to patients and their passions and when she saw me practising yoga in bed, she used that to get me to walk again. She said "Thrust your hips forward, like in yoga!" when I stood for the first time and was a bit wobbly. It worked! And I heard her saying to other patients things like, 'You don't have a high bed at home, do you? How do you usually get out of bed?"

This worked for them and she must have known it wouldn't work for me as she never said it to me, but the problem was, I didn't remember the precise way I got in and out of bed after having been immobile for weeks on end. I just used to do it. There was no considering carefully and then moving. My body just performed the movement for me.

My muscles had now atrophied to an alarming degree (Figure 7.1) and with such speed! Can you remember how precisely you get out of bed? Try it now. Without actually physically moving, describe the precise sequence of movements you make when performing an action, any action, but particularly getting out of bed in the morning. "First I ...", "then ...": go on, try it!

The bars on the bed did help, though. And all that gradual rolling (from at first *being* rolled) from one side to another and holding the bars or a nurse's arms when having a bed bath had definitely helped. And the washing yourself in bed – they used to give me some wipes to wash myself, more and more of my body as I regained movement and it all helped to develop muscles. I progressed from bed baths to sitting down in the shower and being washed to sitting and washing myself, then to standing and washing myself. I remember how exhausted I was after my first shower alone, standing up. They were all important but exhausting steps,

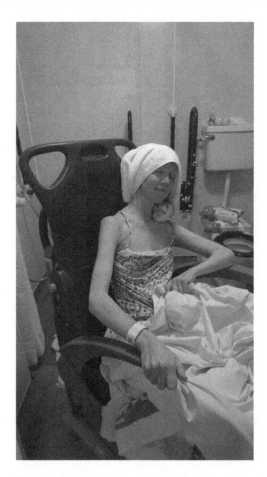

Figure 7.1 Atrophied muscles, sitting in bath chair.

which usually the nurses and physios would understand, but not always. I couldn't lift a hairdryer to my head after showers so when it came to my first time to dry my hair I said to the nurse that this was something I didn't do at home. I did, of course, sometimes, but after this they would never offer me a hairdryer and I never liked to ask. I used to hate the bars on my bed as they reminded me first of a cot, then of a wheelchair. I used to put my hands on them and move them when I could move, in the Lewin – I used to imagine that they were trying to prepare me for lifetime use of a wheelchair – and they squeaked really loudly, much to the annoyance of the three other patients sharing my bay, as they later confirmed.

I remember hearing other patients in my bay yawning and me not being able to do so naturally. I was aware that it was a sign to our bodies to sleep and tried to do it so that I could sleep but was unable physically to yawn (imagine that). I was also unable to shed tears for the first few weeks at least, if not months. I could open my mouth and look like I was crying but couldn't actually shed tears. I can't remember when I was able to cry but I do know I was able to yawn at about two months post-operation. It was a great joy to me! Even now I remember occasionally to consciously enjoy it, that great breath of air, stretching the lungs and chest and then the loud sigh out (if I'm alone or with people who know me well).

But it was more than muscles. Even at home on weekends when I was mobile, I couldn't remember how I used to make simple movements like turning over in bed. I used to complain to Mike that I was uncomfortable and he used to say "Move then!" as if it were the simplest thing in the world. But I couldn't remember how. I would be lying in bed with my head on his chest and didn't seem to be able to exercise the muscle control to lift and turn my head at the same time. I now think it was more the brain–body connection, but at the time it confused me. I was uncomfortable and whereas I used to be able to make myself comfortable effortlessly, I now couldn't. What was happening to me? I was riding a bike, doing yoga and Pilates, and running around in fields but I couldn't move my head!

When I tried to get out the time I allegedly "fell" out of bed I was copying another patient in my bay, who was by that time using a stick to get out of bed and into her wheelchair. I thought I heard the physio or OT say to her, "That's so clever! Crossing one foot over the other like that helps you to get on your feet!" and I thought she (the physio) was deliberately giving me a clue, so I tried it when it was all quiet in the ward one night.

My main aim was not to escape but to show them that I could walk (they weren't letting me have any physio as I had tachycardia[1] at the time). So I hauled myself to the end of my bed with my arms, crossed my feet and fell onto the floor. I remember lying there on my front thinking, "If only I can get onto all fours I can crawl over to those zimmer frames just a few metres away and haul myself up, just like I saw that toddler do in that video", and "narrow window of opportunity, Jel" as the time ticked by. Crawl, then walk: the stages of development, just like those pictures you see on t-shirts of stages of human evolution, usually ending in some comedy pose, hunched over a computer. And then a nurse, or HCA, came past in the wee hours and discovered me lying there on the floor and assumed (rightly in a way) that I'd fallen out of bed. I later agreed with

Mike that I was trying to escape as he thought it was so funny (that I was trying to escape, not that I fell) and am partly writing this for him and the members of my family who still believe the escape story.

I was not in pain at any point that I remember but I was given a vibrating, low air loss bed to reduce the risk of bed sores and to keep my muscles moving. I found it vibrated annoyingly, which I only noticed when I returned to it after a period of time (perhaps from a meal or a trip to the concourse with visitors). It made me feel jittery, which I didn't like, and I thought at the time that this was the bacteria at work again, that my bed was somehow powered by bacteria. Often it would deflate partially or completely, leaving it worse than a normal bed. I later found out, through watching other patients' beds, that this happened when a nurse, patient or visitor knocked one of the switches at the end of the bed. Often the nurses didn't notice so you were left on a kind of a water bed that rolled around and didn't support you. And of course, patients didn't know enough about the beds to realise why they were uncomfortable.

I was desperate not to end up in hospital at the end of my life. I believed, probably mistakenly, that nurses and doctors alike seemed to abandon the elderly unless there was some way of treating them. I thought I overheard a physio on the Lewin Unit once say quietly to another member of staff that another patient in my bay didn't "have rehab potential". She was elderly and had memory issues and there seemed no other option for her family but to put her in a nursing home. Her grandson came to visit once and commented that she was much more fun than before and in fact asked her not to "get sane again"! It was true that she was great fun while her family was there (most evenings) but she would sit in her bed during the whole rest of the day, refusing to come to meals and complaining that none of her family had visited her for ages. She was so sweet though. I thought of her as (and even called her) a dormouse, as my friend Viv had sent me a book on animals and birds which happened to be written by someone at Cambridge, which of course I saw as a sign and started allocating animals and birds to everyone in hospital. Mike's mother, Vera, was a magpie, this other patient was a dormouse, and I allocated new matches and connections for many other people.

In Gawande's *Being Mortal* (2002), there's a particular part that resonated with me. In the chapter on assistance he cites a researcher's study on people's attitude to their elderly relatives: "A colleague once told her, Wilson said, 'We want autonomy for ourselves and safety for those we love'" (p. 106). That's how it sometimes felt to me in hospital and in the BIRT – that I was put there for the comfort of my relatives and partner, or at least for the staff's, that my safety and their fear of litigation came before my autonomy. I felt this when I fell a couple of times on the Lewin Unit, that I was putting the jobs of the staff on duty in jeopardy, and that I had to apologise.

At some point we asked if I could go home at weekends and one of the doctors offered me a deal – weekends at home in exchange for an alarm tag that would go off every time I left the ward. I agreed of course (what else could I do?) but didn't like wearing the tag. I kept it on most weekends, thinking there was some way they could track me (!) but other times I cut it off and had to get a new wristband when I returned on a Sunday evening. Mike couldn't come and pick me up until late morning on a Saturday as he had personal training and usually wanted to take me back by nine or ten on the Sunday. I'm lucky that he's a night owl. Even that was pushing it from the nurses' perspective though. We used to enter the ward, with me saying my hellos to friends among the patients and nurses and trying not to look too smug as I went into my bay and passed the other three patients (who were always glad to see me as we turned the lights off without the nurses' permission) and kissed my beloved goodbye.

Once a staff member came to find me to say I had an appointment down in the Oncology department. I didn't know anything about it as the letter had been sent home and Mike had forgotten to tell me. Indeed, he had forgotten it was happening as it transpired. So this porter arrived with a wheelchair, but I indignantly told him, "I can walk, you know". The nurses let me go as he was with me and we were all sure Mike would join me down there. It seemed odd to be walking beside a man pushing an empty wheelchair, but I went with him down to Oncology and when I arrived was surprised not to see Mike. So was the receptionist and, having told the porter he could go, I told her I was happy to walk back to the Lewin Unit on my own to call Mike and ask him what had happened. The receptionist let me go and I went straight back to the Lewin but I later found out that she telephoned the Lewin to let them know I was on my way up, i.e. to warn them to look for me if I didn't turn up. So mistrustful! (Mind you, I had considered going for a drink on the concourse and enjoying my freedom!) The nurses on the Lewin had to come to look for me in my bay when the call arrived and were surprised to see me there. Mike arrived around half an hour later and we went down together and all was well. I was glad that I had obeyed the rules this time.

I am generally a rule-follower so it was with some surprise that this statement ("I'm a rule abider") was met with raised eyebrows by one of my favourite nurses. I suppose I didn't realise how much my actions were out of character at that time. I had, in previous days at the hospital, run up a staircase without obeying the physio's command to pull the backs of my slippers on, had run around outside when I was supposed to be inside, had gone barefoot contrary to specific and repeated instructions, had "grazed" in the grass outside and eaten various plants, had stretched all the rules because they didn't seem to make any sense. They were just trying to prevent accidents and protect me and I believed the only way to learn was to make mistakes: there's not much room for that in a hospital culture that says it needs to keep patients safe.

I remember Dr Kirker telling me under no circumstances was I to cycle, but I did, on weekends, and hated having to ask Mike's permission. I did start wearing a cycle helmet for the first time though and still do. Mike, of course, was amazing about it and let me, though it would have been him, not me, who would have had to take responsibility had anything happened. He really understood how much my freedom meant to me but even he seemed restrictive to me at times. People would take their cue from him and my friends started saying that I wasn't to cycle and that Mike had trusted them not to let me out of their sight. I referred to this as "babysitting" and they came to too, and although I was happy to see my friends, I resented being watched over the whole time. I remember the morning I got up early and, having left a note for the sleeping Mike and texted him so that he'd see it when he woke up, went to the local park and just walked around and sat under a tree. Ah, bliss! A small piece of real freedom! But I understand now and perhaps I would do the same. I wasn't in my right mind and no one wants to have to deal with the responsibility of an emergency trip to hospital. Now I see Mike and my friends as heroes for "allowing" me my freedom. They were all fantastic at bringing their children along and Sally even let me take her daughter, Bella, to the park on my own on one occasion, playing with her and re-learning how to climb trees. Bella did comment that I wasn't nearly as fast as her mother[2] when we played "spider and fly", a game they had made up on the net climbing frame!

I remember listening to a nurse explaining to another nurse how to remove a catheter and committing it to memory in preparation for an escape. There was one piece that needed to be cut somehow (I've just looked it up and it requires a syringe). I would have to remove my own catheter. I thought about going to my GP – ah no, but he or she would send me straight back to hospital; I'd have to risk infection or ask Mike to do it with a small pair of nail scissors, sterilised of course. I don't know how I thought we could do this, even if Mike had agreed.

Environmental Dependence Syndrome

It's a complex-sounding term for a simple behaviour. I only learned this term when it was used to describe me in a report at the Oliver Zangwill Centre. I had to ask what it meant. It means dependence on environmental clues to the extent of not being able to stop doing something if the occasion or surroundings seem to call for it. Like seeing a toothbrush and compulsively brushing your teeth, even if you were just at the sink to wash your hands and even if it wasn't your toothbrush.

Now I realise why I – and probably other patients – did a lot of things, not just brushing my teeth endlessly. Someone would hold a forkful of food out and I would eat it, even if I was full. Or someone would gesture to the bathroom questioningly and I or another patient would go, even when we didn't need to use the toilet. Body language is a powerful thing and we rely on it more than verbal clues when there is what's known as cognitive dissonance – if someone says to turn left but gestures to the right we will most likely take the right-hand direction.

Perseveration

I remember asking a nurse for earplugs so that I could sleep better at night and him putting them in my ears. I couldn't understand why – I was perfectly capable of rolling them and putting them in my own ears. I only understood when Mike gave me earplugs a couple of weeks later and I couldn't stop rolling them between my fingers until he took them from me and put them in my ears. This was an example of perseveration, which often accompanies SMA Syndrome.

So I often found myself doing things against my will. Someone would offer me a coloured pencil and I would take it. They would plonk a colouring book in front of me and I would be totally absorbed in colouring in, even to the extent of tearing through the page with the pencil. I wouldn't be able to stop until someone took the pencil from me – and often even then I would hold it in a vice-like grip, muscles cramped from the effort of running it back and forth on the page. I think this was influenced by a game on the iPad I'd borrowed, painting without going over the lines.

When a neuropsychologist identified that a good behaviour was to ask me if I wanted to stop and act accordingly, it was such a relief. She told Mike and he told my family and friends, and from then on I felt I was released from torture! I wanted to swap hands but couldn't. I wanted to stop but couldn't. I think part of this was Environmental Dependence

Syndrome but most of it was perseveration. It is the flip side of being unable to initiate something, i.e. the inability to stop doing something.

Confabulation

Confabulation is the putting together of stories (from the root word "fable") that may have come from different memories or simply the imagination and imagining that they're true. For example I once said to an SALT professional that she had not known who the assistant neuropsychologist was. This was completely untrue but I believed it to be true. Misremembering facts and confusing stories (confabulation) became a feature of my SMA Syndrome.

The definition of confabulation contains the phrase, "without the conscious intention to deceive", and I certainly never intended to lie about whatever I was talking about.

Often I would overhear the doctors discussing a patient and they would have the details of his or her case wrong. I sometimes went to put them straight, especially in the later days when I could talk and the patient they were discussing couldn't, only to find that they had been talking about another patient altogether. So convinced was I of "my" truth that I thought they were lying to me!

The BIRT (Brain Injury Rehabilitation Trust)

In one of our "family meetings" on the Lewin Unit it was suggested that my next move on being discharged from this ward might be to the BIRT in Ely. Debs and Mike made a secret and unscheduled visit to see the place and told me it was wonderful and just what I would want. It was, they said, surrounded by fields in which I could roam, full of beautiful gardens in which I could work, and taught clients skills like woodworking – just up my street. The biggest seller was that I'd have my own room. Oh glorious relief! I thought it sounded marvellous and was keen on going as soon as possible. My one caveat was that I wanted to check it out for myself before going. It took rather longer than that to get the discharge team at the Lewin to do its stuff and even longer before Linda Crawford, the manager of the BIRT, would come to do her assessment of me.

When Linda did come to do her assessment she found me in the garden of the Lewin, running up and down the short strip of grass and swinging from the cherry tree, partly because that's how I mostly got my exercise anyway, partly because I was aware she was coming and wanted her to see that I was fully physically able. We sat down inside and she asked me

Figure 7.2 Me in my *huge* private room on my first day at the BIRT.

some questions. She really treated me as a sane individual, an equal, not talking down to me at all, which I really appreciated. I remember saying to her that my motto was "Start before you're ready". She replied that hers was "Slow and steady wins the race"! She commented that the BIRT would have to work hard to keep up with me. I didn't know if she was just flattering me or really felt this. I still don't.

I had believed that Linda would let me come to visit the BIRT before I committed but it didn't work like that. I felt somewhat betrayed by this and thought she had probably just been playing along with my request in order to persuade me to go. But a few long weeks later I was accepted and left the Lewin on a Friday in mid-May 2017, arriving at the BIRT the following Monday (Figure 7.2). Linda had told me – and others had mentioned – that there was another woman on the Lewin who was being assessed at the same time for the BIRT, but that she couldn't tell me who it was. It turned out to be the one I'd shared a four-bed bay with who'd "taught" me that you had to put one foot over the other to walk. The one who I'd annoyed with the rattling of the bed bars, the one who mistook her daughter for her niece and her husband for her brother the first day they had come to visit (whether she really did or not is another matter but it happened for me). But she's not a neuro patient, I thought, she's had a stroke! I didn't understand then that a stroke *was* a neurological problem. I still don't quite understand the distinction between stroke and neuro as most of the beds on the Lewin Unit are for stroke patients, with just four for neuro patients.

The day came when I was to start at the BIRT. Mike dropped me off around midday but first we went for a walk around the centre and the "grounds". I was a little apprehensive, especially as the fields that had been described to me and that I had assumed I could roam freely in, were actually just farmland and inaccessible to patients, who were kept inside at all times and never let out alone. When I discovered this, through seeing a fence around the gym, I burst into tears. I was going to be a prisoner again! The staff thought I was crying because I'd seen the fence and were keen to assure me that it was temporary. But I'd realised I was going to be a prisoner again and it would be worse this time because the visiting hours were much more restricted. Thank goodness for Mike, who came every evening almost without fail for those eight weeks. And when he didn't come, he always made sure someone did in his place. Sometimes I wanted to be alone, but mostly, by the evening, I wanted to be outside. Luckily it was summer and Ely in the summertime is beautiful (Figure 7.3). We would walk in the grounds of the cathedral, go out for dinner or go for a walk along the river and we found this lovely restaurant with a huge garden (Figure 7.4) – it was heaven the first time we went there!

Figure 7.3 Mike and I enjoying the sunshine in Ely.

Figure 7.4 The garden of our favourite restaurant in Ely.

Linda popped in to see me that first day but only briefly so I felt that I was surrounded by strangers, another set of new faces and names to get to know. It was overwhelming at times, trying to navigate these along with the long corridors and three dining rooms. But Linda later told me that this was good for my brain – it releases something called noradrenaline in times of "good" stress. When she told me that, I "embraced the overwhelm".

My first meeting was with a former nurse, now a general art therapist, who buoyed me up with news of all the things I could learn – including knitting (Figure 7.5).

Well, here was a skill I had always wanted to pick up! But unfortunately there were rules around patients having knitting needles so I couldn't practise this new skill in my own room until it was cleared by the powers that be and it took weeks for that to happen. The needles were kept in the art room and I could ask for them any time I wanted but there wasn't any time for this. And I didn't want to bother the art therapist every time as she was so busy. I was only there for eight weeks and permission wasn't granted for me to have needles in my room until my last week.

It was here that I met Sheila, a woman a few years older than me, who'd had a stroke and was now in a wheelchair with spasticity. She had previously been super sporty, a member of her local hockey team and a nutritionist. We bonded over our attitudes – we both believed in a holistic approach to healing and we were both determined to recover. I was reading

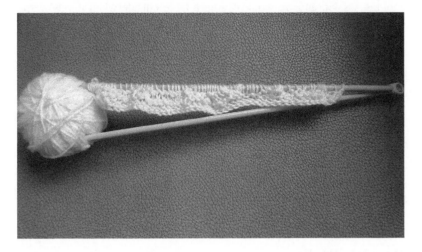

Figure 7.5   Knitting – a fine start.

all sorts of positive stories about recovery, such as those in Doidge's book, *The Brain's Way of Healing* (2016). In it he has a chapter called "Moshe Feldenkrais: Physicist, Black Belt and Healer" in which he quotes Feldenkrais saying, "'Improvement' is a gradual bettering which has no limit. 'Cure' is a return to the previously enjoyed state of activity, which need not have been excellent or even good" (p. 75). I read part of this book to Sheila as some of it concerned healing from strokes; it also helped me with my reading out loud. I've just now read it again (October 2018) and it has a part where he describes a patient for whom recovery was never thought possible: "Everything was to be geared not to fixing her brain but to learning to live with her problems, or to 'compensating' for them, finding ways to work around her limitations" (p. 185). To some extent that's how it felt to me, at the BIRT. I would always be saying, "But I just want to remember naturally as I always have done", and being told that I might never be back to "normal" again so it was better that I learn these compensatory strategies and knuckle down and accept my lot. Or that was the message I heard, anyway.

Sheila and I moaned about the food together – it was better than the hospital food but still not designed to heal and I, much later, in my last few days there, had a run-in with the chef. We used to cook together at lunchtime when we were allowed to. Sheila had a wonderful OT called Gemma, who later appeared at the Oliver Zangwill Centre (but that's another story). Gemma would allow me into the kitchen when Sheila was having a cooking session and we would lay up a table outside when it was warm enough and eat together. I don't know what the other patients and staff thought of us but we were happy. Sheila is now making what she calls "slow progress" but progress nonetheless. She's using something called a FitMi from the USA, a rehab system linked to a computer, which gives her thousands of repetitions of exercises to do. The last time I heard from her she said she was in tears as she realised she could suddenly actively lift her foot off the ground to do one of the exercises (10,000 repetitions). Her arm was more able and hand less spastic and she was "walking" the dog in the woods in her electric wheelchair. Progress indeed, my friend! She later reported (via email in April 2019) that "I am still working with the FitMi. I am way ahead on what I can do before fatigued, but as ever frustrated at progress. Been working on meditation and mindfulness. I am feeling much more grounded."

Maggie's Wallace

I started going to Maggie's Wallace at the behest of Mike, who'd seen signs for it on his travels around Addenbrooke's. We went together the first time and I loved it from the first meeting with one of the counsellors. She had been a neuro-nurse and had seen SMA Syndrome before so totally understood that at that time I found eye contact too difficult to manage. I had my eyes closed for most of the conversation, which anyone else would have found odd, but she didn't. I went to the therapies and yoga offered, enjoyed the lovely, comfortable atmosphere and even a monthly brain tumour support group. One of the counsellors, Aneesh, had worked at the Oliver Zangwill Centre and had also seen SMA Syndrome before. He recommended that I go to OZC as they might be able to help me. He described it as "the next level up from the BIRT".

I read the book by Maggie Keswick-Jencks (1995), the founder of Maggie's, later and found it truly inspiring – so much of what she says in there resonates with me, I could have written the words myself. She believed we should not "lose the joy of living in the fear of dying" and that cancer patients should be informed participants in their medical treatment and receive stress-reducing strategies, psychological support and the opportunity to meet people in similar circumstances in a relaxed domestic setting. The Maggie's Wallace centre at Addenbrooke's hospital is just such a place where you can access the latest information on cancer, not be judged for trying alternative treatments like cannabis oil and naturopathy, receive therapies like massage, Reiki and reflexology, participate in activities like yoga and meditation and get access to counselling, all for free. I went at least once a week and sometimes every couple of days during my radiotherapy and for a while later, and bought a number of stylish caps there (the first one was free) and got a wig (again for free) when my hair started falling out, which I only wore on special occasions as I didn't enjoy "faking it" too often. I reasoned that if I looked like I had hair it would be more of a shock to people when I had it cut off. I wanted to be "real", but I did enjoy wearing it out.

I remember my friend, Sally, accompanying me to one counselling session at which I didn't know what I was doing and her saying how impressed she was by the place and the counsellor. She also did me a huge favour, as I told her at the time, by telling the counsellor how unlike myself I was in being so confused. In reality I'm sure the counsellor knew this, but having Sal there, an obviously highly intelligent, professional woman, shone some reflected light on me as a person, her friend.

Amchara

I went to a retreat called Amchara in Somerset immediately after radio-therapy, which had been recommended by my naturopath and researched by Debs, my sister. Debs telephoned and emailed in advance to make sure they could meet my many needs for raw food and detoxing, including colonic irrigation, enemas and saunas. I wasn't there so much for the information sessions that they held once a day on issues such as hypnosis, CBT (cognitive behavioural therapy) or for the informative films that they showed each evening, as for the raw food and care I could receive there – someone else to meet my basic needs so that I could focus fully on recovery and take the pressure off Mike for a while. I went to the yoga classes each day and spent lots of time out walking in the local fields. Debs came for 10 days towards the end and Tab came for a couple of days. My dad visited for a day, as did another friend and Mike came for the last couple of days.

Otherwise I was alone for the six weeks, which I loved, after being with other people and watched over for so long. I wasn't at the stage of watch-ing films or reading books, but I did appreciate the freedom of being able to sleep when I wanted and being able to get massages and Reiki daily. There were beautiful gardens where butterflies flew about and a pond with grasses overhanging it and flowers everywhere, including buddleia plants and several huge yew trees entwined with each other. Other guests were surprised to hear that I was staying that long as they were only there typic-ally for five to seven days. I felt very fortunate to be in this place, but slightly alone at mealtimes, even when there were other people present. I couldn't yet cope with other people, but by the time my sister came I was already so much better.

Staff, too, were amazed at the difference in me between my first and last week. This was partly due to time and partly to the healing I was getting from the combination of raw food, supplements, enemas and fresh air and plants. I used to go for daily walks in the wildlife sanctuary (really just fields and a small forest but a protected area with horses running wild), and when Debs came out we would go for runs together (she was doing "a mile a day in May").

Authentic movement and breathwork

Jane Okondo,[3] a breathwork practitioner and movement specialist, with whom I'd had sessions and workshops while living in London and who had become a friend, came to visit me at the BIRT and later at home in Cambridge. When she came to the BIRT in May 2017, I was so happy to see her – at last! Someone who knew and understood me and my "strange ways"! I wanted to shout aloud for joy and introduce her to everyone. But I didn't. I curled up in her arms on the bed and cried like a baby. And it felt so good. She was so accepting and caring; she held me for the longest time and witnessed me move. Witnessing is an important thing in authentic movement, which is the field Jane works in among others. She and I had been together to a Somatic Conference, somatic meaning to do with the body rather than the mind, and it had been a pivotal part of my Master's dissertation. I asked her whether she had trained in another practitioner's technique, Peter Levine's Somatic Experiencing, and she said that she had but could use any technique I liked. In the end we didn't use any technique (well, I'm sure we did but not consciously so) and just moved together.

She was then on her way to a gathering of somatic practitioners including my teachers from Body and Earth (a movement workshop run at Schumacher College and designed by Andrea Olsen to connect the human body with the earth body) and she said she would remember me to them. I later (much later) booked myself onto a retreat with the same team and they remembered me. It was wonderful to move the way my body wanted to.

Butterflies and signs

At some point I became aware that I was seeing butterflies everywhere – images on the journal that someone had given me, on the walls, in the colouring books I was given, on the neighbours' bedsheets hung up to dry when I went home at weekends, everywhere! When butterfly season began and there were actually live butterflies it was the same. At Amchara there was a butterfly in the garden on a buddleia bush immediately as Mike and I walked around, butterfly prints in my room (and no other room, as I later discovered) and even, later, when I was alone, a butterfly flew out of the wardrobe and roosted for the night in the bathroom. There were whole hosts of butterflies in the nearby meadows too; this was an obvious thing as they were feeding at this time on the meadow flowers but they delighted me. Purple flowers seemed to be everywhere too, and the buddleia bush particularly attracted me – the plant that butterflies typically congregate around.

A friend later told me that butterflies were a symbol of transformation and reminded me that purple was the colour of the crown chakra. I did feel that a major transformation was on its way, but didn't recognise that it was already happening until Marlow, my homeopath, pointed it out in a session.

Hypnotherapy

Tab, one of my best friends, talked to another friend of mine, Viv Hill, who I'd met at Schumacher College, a hypnotherapist who'd previously recorded what I found to be a very helpful hypnotherapy session. She said she was happy to make me another and I wanted one for radiotherapy so Tab briefed Viv and Viv recorded a special hypnotherapy session for me which centred on me being in a garden, surrounded by butterflies and a buddleia bush. She suggested that I see the radiotherapy beams as beams of gratitude – "you're grateful for them and they're helping you". This really helped me to see the radiotherapy as benign if not healing.

The Oliver Zangwill Centre (OZC)

This was probably the best rehabilitation centre I attended. Maybe because I was ready for it, maybe because I could come and go independently, by train and taxi, who knows, but it was. It was due to a series of coincidences that I got in at all. First, Aneesh from Maggie's Wallace had spoken about it; then Mike and I met Andrew Bateman, the clinical lead of OZC, at the Cambridge Science Festival. Then we asked Dr Kirker about it and he promised to have a word with OZC.

Mike and I kept pressing and pressing for an assessment at every meeting with an Addenbrooke's clinician until I finally got an assessment date, in October 2017. It was supposed to be over two days but I had mine in one. They said they'd let me know. I remember meeting Dr Jessica Fish, who has since left, and being uncharacteristically reserved with her. I also met Sue Brentnall, head of occupational therapy, for a test on the computer, which I thought I'd sailed through with ease, although I guessed the time it had taken incorrectly when she asked me. It helped that it was based on a planned visit to London, a city I knew well, though she didn't know this when she'd set the test up.

I was a bit unsure about my need for this programme, so I think I came across as both mentally unstable and incredibly stable at the same time. This ambivalence was a ruse to get me in but let the staff know I didn't *really* need to be there. I was aware that I was changing day to day and didn't have the same needs from one day to the next. I think I seemed a bit arrogant. I wouldn't have let me in but the staff at the Oliver Zangwill Centre have seen it all before. To be honest, I don't think I knew what I wanted, but Mike was enthusiastic about it. If he hadn't wanted me to go there, I probably wouldn't have gone. (Or perhaps it would have made me want to go even more!)

I started the six-week intensive programme on 8 January 2018. The first day I met the rest of my cohort: Craig, Lee and Mark. Craig – who has sadly now passed away, though not from his brain injury – had been run into by a car while he was cycling, which had left him with a brain injury; Lee had had a similar accident driving his horse and carriage; Mark had had a brain tumour, like me, albeit of a different type in a different part of his brain. Though we had sustained different injuries in different ways, the symptoms were remarkably similar. Uncharacteristic aggression, mood swings, disinhibition, it was all there to varying degrees in all of us. But as I came to understand at OZC, no two brain injuries are the same, even if they are sustained in the same way and in the same area of the brain. We are different people to start off with, with different life experiences, attitudes, values and cognitive abilities.

The OZC produces a one-page document called a *formulation* to describe each client based on interviews with the patient and his or her family. I felt mine summed me up surprisingly well: it describes the person you were pre-brain injury, which given the staff hadn't known me pre-brain injury was pretty good. (The formulation can be seen in Chapter 13, Figure 13.1.)

Mood swings

I had huge mood swings in hospital and throughout my recovery. At first I couldn't feel emotions apart from fear/distress and their counter emotions, hope/excitement. I swung from one to the other wildly. As I started to recover however, the range of emotions I could feel became slowly broader and more complex. I was moody, angry, irritated, frustrated and also relatively calm, happy and excited. But I was swinging between these all the time and tears – once I *could* cry – were pretty much a constant. At the Oliver Zangwill Centre something my whole cohort had in common was rudeness or irritability or even anger towards those we loved and it was out of character for all of us. One of us in particular, a client called Lee, suffered from anger outbursts which he'd never experienced before to the same extent. He had had the police round on a few occasions, which had also never happened before the brain injury. His wife and daughter were at the end of their tethers and, when he was part-way through the programme and implementing some of the anger management strategies we'd all been taught, he proudly showed us a text from his wife, which read along the lines of "I feel like I've got the old you back".

This may have been due to lack of sleep caused by our brain injuries but also by being hospitalised for substantial periods of time. As Matthew Walker (2017), author of *Why We Sleep*, reports of an experiment he performed:

The amygdala, a key hotspot for triggering strong emotions such as anger and rage ... showed well over a 60% amplification in emotional reactivity in the participants who were sleep deprived. In contrast the brain scans of those individuals who were given a full night of sleep evinced a controlled, modest degree of reactivity in the amygdala, despite viewing the very same images. It was as though, without sleep, our brain reverts to a primitive pattern of uncontrolled reactivity. We produce unmetered, inappropriate emotional reactions and are unable to place events into a broader or more considered context.

Why were the emotion centres of the brain so excessively reactive without sleep?

After a full night of sleep, the prefrontal cortex – the region of the brain that sits just above your eyeballs and is most developed in humans relative to other primates and is associated with rational, logical thought and decision making – was strongly coupled to the amygdala, regulating this deep emotional brain centre with inhibitory control. With a full night of plentiful sleep, we have a balanced mix between our emotional gas pedal (amygdala) and brake (prefrontal cortex). Without sleep, however, the strong coupling between these two brain regions is lost. ... Without the rational control given to us each night by sleep we're not on a neurological and hence emotional even keel.

(p. 124)

This explained why I was so up and down emotionally. On top of the brain injury, I wasn't getting enough sleep in the hospital. That was why going home at weekends was so beneficial to me. But the thing with sleep is, as Matthew Walker explains, that there is no effective way to catch up on it. Ever. Once you've lost a night of sleep you can never get it back. The theory that you can have "catch-up" sleep, either on weekends or at any other time, is a myth and this is backed up by numerous scientific studies.

The programme at OZC was as follows:

> Week 1: Induction, during which there was the first Family Day, to which my dad and Mike came
> Week 2: UBI (Understanding Brain Injury)
> Week 3: Attention and Memory
> Week 4: Communication
> Week 5: Executive Function
> Week 6: Mood

The best part of every week was when I would learn something that told me I was "normal". Sometimes it would happen several times in one day. For example, during the first week we were told that when there's a discrepancy between the person you used to be and the person you are now, the limbic system kicks in – the emotional body – and I thought aha! This explains my "toddler state" of high emotion!

Later on, while I was writing this book, I overheard a conversation on the street between a mother and her toddler. Her toddler was wailing and the mother said, "I don't understand – please use words". I thought, "That's exactly what Mike and my family used to say to me!" But I couldn't at the time find the words to describe what I was feeling and what I wanted. Perhaps I couldn't even formulate the thoughts.

During Executive Function week I learned about the causes of my personal difficulties and I heard that these are not personality flaws – what a relief that was! There are four domains to executive function, which is dealt with by the frontal lobes (damaged in my case by the operation). There are several things under each domain that might have changed. These are shown in Table 7.1.

We learned that damage to one's frontal lobes, i.e. executive function, leads to loss of the abstract attitude, coming at things from the wrong perspective and failure to adapt. This was music to my ears as I'd experienced all of this and thought it was just me. There are several things that can make it worse, such as people talking to you as you're trying to do something (I'd had that), TV or radio on in the background while you're trying

Table 7.1 The four domains to executive function

Domain	What others see or what you might see
ENERGISATION: doing things	You: Do I just not care anymore?
	Others: Has she lost her lust for life?
EXECUTIVE COGNITION: thinking, problem solving, prioritisation	You: Am I just stupid now?
	Others: She's so rigid!/She's so black and white!
EMOTIONAL: behavioural self-regulation, feeling, acting	You: Have I become an out-of-control freak?
	Others: She's so out of control/dysregulated!
METACOGNITION: awareness and socialising	You: Could there be something wrong that I don't know about, or is it just them?
	Others: (a range of things including, for me personally, She's changed so much! She's so withdrawn now, so inward-looking!)

to think (yes), time pressure (mmhmm), or being tired, anxious, in pain or over-excited (bingo). Finally! This explained so much!

There were strategies, too, that could help. I mostly devoured these and learned a lot from them. One concerned loss of emotional control, which I experienced a lot. We reviewed where emotions were dealt with in the brain: many areas but including the amygdala, which is part of the limbic system and which dictates fight, flight or freeze (I knew these three but was later introduced to a fourth "f" by my herbalism teacher, which is the "fawn" response, i.e. appeasing the other); the hypothalamus, mostly hormonal; the insular cortex, which is where understanding and interpreting body sensations happens; parts of the frontal lobe (logic, reasoning); and the temporal lobes (memory).

There are two routes to emotion: one is quick and automatic (the amygdala) and one is slower and takes account of previous experiences, via the frontal lobes and hippocampus. The example we were asked to consider is that you're walking down the street and someone you know doesn't stop to talk to you. Your amygdala immediately kicks in with an indignant response such as "Hey! She/he ignored me!" Normally your frontal lobes might tell you, "Calm down, they just didn't see you, they were too engrossed in their own thoughts." Your hippocampus might relay information about all the times this has happened before – and when it hasn't. But in brain injury your amygdala rules and you get angry.

The bit that I was interested in was how to *control* your emotions as I mostly had been able to before. The advice given was twofold:

> Understand and, if appropriate, apologise.
> Recognise early signs of rising emotions.

Strategies included: Stop, Think and the GMF (Goal Management Framework) in the immediate term; staying calm and promoting the state of your parasympathetic nervous system in the long term, by meditating, breathing, for me doing yoga nidra etc.

Some strategies I was resistant to on principle (that I would have to use specific strategies at all) and others I realised I already used without having defined them as strategies. One of these was something that OZC taught as the Goal Management Framework (Robertson, 1996; Levine et al., 2000). It sounds fancy, doesn't it? "Let's GMF it!" was the rallying cry. Here's how it works in six stages:

> What is my GOAL?
> What are my possible SOLUTIONS?
> List the pros and cons of each until you come to a DECISION
> Steps to get there = a PLAN
> DO it
> REVIEW it – EVALUATE

I realised that, although I didn't write it down, I had already used this strategy automatically to weigh up my options and decide on a course of action. The value of writing it down was that I actually realised what steps these were and thought of more options than I would have been able to do just mentally. I rarely evaluated it in practice though – too much effort!

Days at OZ, as I came to know it, started with a community meeting with all staff and clients in the centre that day – and someone would announce who would be coming in later. The purpose was always clearly stated if there were any newcomers in the room, and intros made enough times so that by the end of the first week I knew or had at least heard everyone's names. The role of chair was rotated according to volunteers, as were other "chores" such as collecting the milk from the canteen and emptying and refilling the dishwasher, feeding the fish, walking the therapy dog (oh yes, there was a therapy dog, whose role was also sometimes rotated!) and so on. It was similar to what I had experienced at Schumacher College's morning Community Meeting, though smaller and around a table, and birthdays would be celebrated, duties and tasks allocated and ticked off, and an "item of interest" provided rather than a reading. It was a lovely way to start the day and soon the place started to feel like home.

After the morning meeting and a tea break we had sessions together as a group from 11.30 until 12.15 which were on the topic for the week. The 45-minute duration had been arrived at as it's about the longest a person with a brain injury can concentrate for. Indeed, it's the longest most people can concentrate for, if receiving new information. The first week the session consisted of an overview of the programme, sharing stories, group rules, outcomes, planning the family day, expectations of rehab, fatigue and a trip to Ely. This was all really important as it got us settled in to the place and to each other. We were treated respectfully and our needs and aims listened to, which was a pleasant surprise, having been treated differently at Addenbrooke's and to some extent at the BIRT. During this week we met the previous cohort who all came across, despite individual difficulties, as perfectly normal people (what did I expect?).

During the afternoons we had individual sessions with therapists, who might be the people who delivered the content for the morning session or an OT or your IPC (individual programme co-ordinator), all of whom had been identified in the pre-admission folder we had been sent in the post. One of them – Hermione – had been on the Speech and Language team at Addenbrooke's and although I hadn't worked directly with her there, it was comforting to see a familiar face. There were sessions on Mood, OT, SALT, IPC – I already knew most of these acronyms but IPC was a new one on me. I soon grew to use it as the others did without thinking of its full form, individual programme co-ordinator. There were also "visiting scholars" from Japan (a neurosurgeon called Aoki) and Iran (a psychologist called Zoleikha), which added nicely to the multiculturalism and collaboration.

I undertook a series of established tests, mostly with Pieter, my individual programme co-ordinator (IPC), who was also my mentor during Cog (Cognitive) sessions, but also with Sue and Hermione. Dr Jessica Fish (Jess) was my favourite and I used to have Mood sessions with her that were really free and open to anything I wanted to discuss. My own therapist for free! We really bonded during those few weeks and although she left the OZC at the end of September 2018, we said we'd stay in touch, with her promising to give me her personal email address, which I finally obtained in January 2019.

I was lucky enough to meet the Oliver Zangwill Centre's founder, Professor Barbara Wilson, a renowned neuropsychologist. She's a giant of a woman and by that I don't mean in stature (she's petite) but in efficiency. Pieter used to say to me, when he was trying to convince me to use a memory system, "Barbara uses a Filofax and if even Barbara has to use a system, we all should be using systems!"

At some point Barbara suggested that I write a chapter for her series on surviving brain injury – I was under the impression that she wanted a chapter but she meant a book. At that point, in her seventies and officially retired, though still racing around the world speaking and writing about brain injury, she was about to publish her 27th book, so who was I to argue? Besides, I wanted to do it, partly as therapy and for a sense of purpose and partly because I've always wanted to write. And who wouldn't be attracted by the idea of being a published author? I did, however, want to change the title of the series from Survivors Series to Thrivers Series, even if just for this account. Obviously this was *not* accepted! I am in no doubt that Routledge accepted the book proposal on her reputation, and certainly all the interviews and the involvement of everyone from my surgeon to my former speech and language therapist at Addenbrooke's are down to her influence. If Barbara says she'll do something, you know it will get done. And she's so modest and unassuming and kind, which is a really attractive combination of traits. She reminds me of my housemistress at school, full of no-nonsense wisdom.

Following the six-week intensive (Monday to Thursday) programme, there were 12 weeks of a continuing programme which consisted of two days a week, consisting of more individual therapy and tests and putting what we had learned into practice. It also featured a project called "Understanding Brain Injury", during which we received an expert overview of our brain scans from Aoki, the Japanese scholar and neurosurgeon, and were given the chance to ask questions that we might not have done of our surgeons or clinical team at the hospital. At the end of this project clients are given the opportunity to do a piece of work of their choice, which might be a picture, a sculpture or a short article on their understanding of brain injury, to cement the learning. Mine is this book.

There was also a weekly support group during these 12 weeks, which I loved. Our cohort would get together with a therapist (who sometimes rotated depending on availability, which again I appreciated as it gave us a chance to experience different people) and talk about whatever was coming up in our lives. It was a chance to say whatever we wanted. The support of the group was often more important than anything the therapist would say, though the staff played a skilful facilitation role.

Mike and I later had relationship counselling from another counsellor, Leyla Prince, which was extraordinarily helpful and enabled us to go our separate ways with love. We performed a ceremony that was really helpful too, at the suggestion of Marlow, my homeopath, which involved asking if we wanted to continue this relationship and blessing what it had been. We were both undecided at this point – before the counselling – but it was a beautiful beginning for the ending.

Mike maintains that my personality changed after the radiotherapy but I think it's more that the naturopathic regime started then (raw food, supplements and enemas) and I was so regimented about it that it caused friction between us. For example, I had to do two enemas a day, each with a hot bath beforehand. Since we timed the radiotherapy for the late afternoons so that Mike could drive me without taking too much time off from work, I would have a hot bath and enema pretty much immediately after we got home, which was around dinner time. He didn't like this, especially when his mother was visiting which coincided with the first few days of radiotherapy, and I wouldn't have liked it either, but I had to get it done before I went to bed. Then there was that we couldn't just go out for dinner or stop somewhere along the way for food – my food always had to be planned. I am relaxing quite a bit now but then it seemed too important – and much easier to follow a set of strict rules than to make up my own way and to depart from it. Anyway, we were both going in new directions and too hampered by the other to continue our relationship. We had become like loving housemates and that's no substitute for a relationship.

At some point Gemma, from the BIRT, appeared at OZC. Remember her from earlier? She was the one who bent the rules to allow Sheila and I to cook together. It was so good to see her – she had got a job as a rehabilitation assistant at the OZC. I remembered her to Sheila in an email and they each sent the other their best wishes.

One day we were asked to prepare for a kind of Dragon's Den session: to prepare a presentation on something we wanted to introduce for the Oliver Zangwill Centre. I decided to apply for funding for an online game I'd read about that promised to train the brain for improvement in conditions like brain injury and autism. It sounded ace!

The problem with most online games for the brain, according to OZC was that they only trained you in that particular game, but this one promised to have spill-over effects into real life. I got myself into trouble as the book hadn't fully explained the game and its benefits and I needed to do some online research. Not only were the computers and connection extremely slow at OZC but I had to get my head around and put into a presentation entirely new material – and to be able to field questions about it – in the space of a couple of days. I had a session the next day with Pieter and confessed to being quite stressed about it.

But I wanted to do a good job and, as usual, thought someone else's words and ideas would be better than mine. He talked me through it and found that what I was really interested in was natural building and skills sharing. I talked so passionately about building a cob oven that he persuaded me to do my Dragon's Den on this instead. I extended it to skills sharing of all kinds and was able to use photos of the time when I ran a cob oven building session with a small team of people (Figure 7.6).

The actual presentation in front of a small team of staff and someone from our cohort went well and the idea was generally accepted by the OZC team and clients later in a vote on which ideas should be implemented (result: all of them). However, from the point of needing to implement it I became frustrated because it would clearly need to be taken on by staff in order to work as we were almost at the end of the programme and I couldn't see this happening. They were all so overworked and a new cohort would soon arrive and want to do their own thing, so I dumped the

Figure 7.6 Building a cob oven in 2016.

idea. But Pieter was right – I needed to present something I actually knew about and could speak passionately about, not someone else's words and ideas that I only had shady knowledge of.

With Pieter I did a test called the Towers Test and I was bad at it and in the feedback session looking for and excited at the possibility of finding some meta-formula for working things out. All things. As if there were such a thing. But I was holding out for it. I got upset, really upset, when I found there was none.

I found I was always looking for the silver bullet, a solution that would solve everything. I was excited to read about each new development in cognitive research in books by Norman Doidge (2016) and others. And yet one of my key learnings in hospital had been that no one solution is good for absolutely everyone. There is no one-size-fits-all solution, whether pharmaceutical or psychological/therapeutic. Everyone responds to things differently.

Notes

1 Tachycardia (when your heart beats abnormally fast) is normally 100 beats per minute (bpm) + for adults. Mine was sometimes going at 130 bpm.
2 Sally did compete in the 800 m Masters for GB in 2018, coming seventh in the world, so perhaps this is not surprising!
3 Jane has a company called Soma Flow: www.somaflow.okwellbeing.com

Chapter 8

Naturopathy and strategies that have helped

Alex Jelly

While I was at the BIRT I started trying to find an alternative to radiotherapy. It seemed such a blunt instrument to me. I found a naturopath who specialised in cancer treatment through my sister Debs. This naturopath worked out of London as well as Ireland and did phone and Skype consultations.

You will recall from earlier that I was in rehab at the BIRT with a woman called Sheila who'd had a stroke. She used to be a nutritionist and knew a senior nutritionist, her former tutor, upon whom she relied to prescribe supplements. So when I found this naturopath I asked Sheila if she'd heard of her. She said she hadn't, but her friend/tutor might have done. I emailed him and he replied, full of praise for her, and said if he had a wife or sister going through cancer he would send her to this naturopath without hesitation. It was all about signs for me in those days, so that did it for me. I booked a Skype call for as soon as possible and my sister Debs joined us. I couldn't really take in much information at that stage so Debs was there to help me understand.

This doctor was my naturopath until early 2019 when I sought other help as she wasn't delivering on administrative things such as sending test results back in time for consultations, and was taking up too much time in consultations going over what supplements I was on – to my mind she should have had this information on file and readily available, whether this was reasonable or not.

So I changed naturopaths and again my sister – who by this time was well into her Functional Medicine course at the College of Natural Medicine – was my best source of information. She recommended two naturopaths who specialised in cancer and I contacted both of them with the same email. One of them turned out to be a Functional Medicine Practitioner and the first thing she did was to send me for a gut test, which had some interesting results, such as that I wasn't absorbing all the good fats I was putting in my body and that I had something called SIBO – Small Intestinal Bacterial Overgrowth – which she is now treating.

Homeopathy – Marlow Purves

As mentioned before, when I thought I was depressed my friend, Anna, recommended her homeopath, Marlow Purves, who was such a wonderful find. She's become a friend as well as my homeopath and often visited me in the hospital without charging me. She's kind and perceptive and always has a smile ready to hand, not to mention her magic remedies. I remember her telling me that you could make a remedy out of anything, even a poem or a song. She was making one that weekend with some friends out of a particular mineral or stone.

So I told her my favourite poem of that time – it was by Daniel Ladinsky and inspired by a fourteenth-century Persian Sufi poet called Hafiz (Wikiquote, n.d.) – and asked her to make a remedy out of it:

Even after all this time the sun never says to the Earth, "You owe me."
Look what happens with a love like that. It lights up the whole world.

She told me just to say it out loud, with feeling, and it would be a remedy in itself. It was.

In the days when I couldn't work out how I was feeling she would often suggest something and it would always hit the nail on the head. (It still happens now.)

Herbalism – Nathaniel Hughes

I had been seeing a herbalist – who has developed a very intuitive way of working – near Stroud for some time before the brain tumour. I was looking for a plant teacher and found Nathaniel Hughes through recommendations. After trying a few others who I didn't really connect with, I found Nathaniel to be wonderfully genuine, modest and effective. He had a chemistry background yet he didn't think he knew it all. Instead, he was guided by the plants, constantly learning from direct experience, the way I wanted to.

Similarly to Stephan Harding, my tutor at Schumacher College, Nathaniel knew there was more to plants than science could teach and had opened to them after a period of depression in his twenties, finding solace in the herbs around him. He was – and still is – really interested in the plants of the British Isles and our own Pagan/Druid traditions, which have been buried by various religions and the state over the centuries. I went to see him for my UTI but really it was to learn about plants from him, which I told him in our first session.

He happened to telephone me a few days before the operation asking whether we had booked an appointment (we hadn't, to my knowledge), and I told him about the upcoming operation. I then emailed him from the Lewin one day many months later and spoke to him a few days after that. I was in my "no filters" stage and so was very direct with him, which he (refreshingly!) found refreshing.

I'd been drawn to "grazing" on the grass at the hospital, munching away at the dandelions and other plants, much to the dismay of Mike and also of my friend, Bron, who was visiting that day. She was heavily pregnant at the time, and couldn't physically stop me or lift me up when I couldn't get up. She actually did me a favour as I was able to get up from the grass on my own (Mike had gone to get drinks for us all). I borrowed a strategy from the physiotherapist who would sometimes give me private yoga classes (she was also a qualified Iyengar yoga teacher), who had told me just to kneel and then put weight down through my legs. Once word got out about my eating of the plants the nurses were drafted in to stop me. Nathaniel later told me that he'd had his group of herbalism students grazing on dandelions too – I believe we were psychically connected, as I had been with Jane.

Cherry was an important and special tree for me (I had found healing through her before) and it was magnificent to find a cherry tree in the garden that I could access most of the time when I was finally walking and trusted to go outside on my own into the garden beside the Lewin. And it was the tree to which I turned on my first meeting from the hospital with Mike's mother, Vera, who I called my "mother-in-love", as Mike and I weren't married, taking the term from Karolyne, who called her partner (my friend John)'s mother the same. I hugged a cherry tree down by the River Cam and she (Vera) later sent me a cherry tree, which I cherish (see what I did there?)

My friend Anna and I later walked in the Jubilee Gardens and made up names for all the plants – much better than their common names – after a plant teacher at Schumacher exhorted us to "call each plant by its [12] names" to distract us from thinking about their "known" properties or attributes. The name so often gets in the way of the thing. For example, a marigold might become "Sun Worshipper" and a yew tree "Great Spiny One".

Nathaniel joined my "Team Jelly", consisting thus far of Marlow and Jane, so now I had a herbalist on board too. He and Marlow discussed what homeopathic remedies I was on over the phone and decided together on a course of treatment with herbs and remedies that wouldn't negatively interact with each other.

Nathaniel supported me by diving into the research and became my "go-to" guy for all things research related, as well as my advisor and supporter on plant teas and remedies. He suggested a smoothie to make in the mornings at the BIRT with nut milk, frankincense (to cross the blood–brain barrier) and turmeric (an anti-inflammatory), combined with black pepper to help the body absorb the other ingredients. I brought along my own "Nutri Ninja" blender one weekend from home for this purpose and was allowed to keep it in my room. It made a terrible noise and I was worried it would disturb other clients/patients; a few times it caused the fire doors to close with the vibrations!

One weekend off from Addenbrooke's, I went walking with Mike and Tab in the Magog Hills beyond Cambridge and we found a whole field of cowslips (Figure 8.1), some of which I picked along with other flowers, just allowing myself to be led by the plants. I gathered a small bouquet which I took to my homeopathy session following the walk to show Marlow. I also reported to Nathaniel which flowers and plants I'd been drawn to, and he recommended going to do a meditation with the cowslips and making tea from them too, which I later did.

One thing that appeared to have good evidence behind it was the medicinal mushroom, Reishi, combined with citrus juice or fruit. But I was already taking Reishi in homeopathic form so couldn't at that time take it in its material form. I did later and still do now.

Figure 8.1 Cowslips.

The risks of the radiotherapy were numerous. My old symptoms (headaches and vomiting) might worsen during radiotherapy. I might experience sleepiness, poor appetite or lack of energy. Damage to the hippocampus could result in memory loss; the pituitary gland that controls the hormones throughout the body could be irreparably damaged, causing anything from reduced sex drive to thyroid problems. Also a second brain tumour was a risk, albeit small. Here's what Cancer Research UK (n.d.) has to say about it:

> In very rare cases, you may develop another brain tumour many years after you were first treated. This is because, although radiation kills cancer cells, it is also a risk factor for developing them.
>
> Unfortunately, tumours caused by previous radiotherapy tend not to respond very well to treatment. The tumours might be high grade and grow more quickly.

At the time of writing I'm still within the first two years of treatment so I don't know whether I will develop a second tumour – fingers crossed!

Having read all these symptoms you can understand why I was reluctant to just go for it with radiotherapy, but I eventually found my peace with it and decided to do it *alongside* the naturopathic diet and regime of supplements and enemas.

Every weekday for six weeks I was to go to Addenbrooke's for radiotherapy. I started in mid-July 2017. I had been fitted with a mask which was quite a pleasant feeling as they warm it up so that they can mould it to your face and it feels almost like a facial (Figure 8.2).

Mike and I joked about me going into a spa. They wanted to deliver high-energy radiation to my head, so couldn't have the head moving about during treatment. I'm lucky that I don't get claustrophobic as apparently some patients find it almost unbearable being inside the radiotherapy machine, let alone having the mask fitted. The radiotherapy machine is like an MRI scanner, a tunnel you get moved into from the front but it's open at the back as well. It makes horrendously loud noises and vibrations and sounds like it's going round your whole body, although I was assured it wasn't. I also saw flashing lights every time, apparently just a result of the stimulation of my optic nerves.

It was lucky we lived so close to the hospital as Mike could take me there almost every day. My wonderful friend Tab set up the idea of guardian angels to accompany me into each radiotherapy session. I would have two each day, enough to focus on and a channel for everyone else's love. People would sign up for a specific day (I think Tab used an app for

Figure 8.2 The hospital "spa".

this) and she would tell me, or the app would, who were my angels for that day. Often Tab or my angels would get in touch directly with me on the appropriate day.

I remember the first day of radiotherapy, as Mike drove me to hospital, I wore his mother's purple pashmina, had with me a felted purple butterfly that a friend's daughter, Mia, had made for me, and was listening to a meditation CD that a friend's mother had given me. The meditation CD, which we listened to in the car, was a prayer for love and health for yourself and for a good friend. This was perfect as I had my two oldest friends, Bron and Claire, as my guardian angels for that first day. I wished them love and perfect health and, as I did, I felt a weight drop from me. It was as if I couldn't direct love towards myself but I could feel it by directing it towards them.

I also had Barbara Fernandez, the "Rocking Raw Chef" to bring me raw food every couple of days and juices too. My sister Debs had found her to help me through those first few weeks of a raw food diet, as I had plenty else on my plate, not to mention still being in cognitive recovery. Barbara was a real inspiration and made and recommended delicious things for me to eat, foods that protected me from radiation (such as seaweed and juices that would help me detox) and foods that were good for the brain (including avocados, fermented foods like kimchi, sauerkraut etc., coconut oil, nuts, seeds, green leafy veg and so on). I can't thank her enough as I really didn't have the brain power, organisation or knowledge to feed myself during this difficult time. She also introduced me to the "Dirty Dozen" and the "Clean Fifteen", not her own list but a widely available list of which foods retain most and least pesticide residue. This was created for the US market and there's no equivalent that I can find for the UK, but I suppose it's broadly similar.

I used to eat organically for the environment – I already understood how persistent the chemicals we now spray on crops were to the environment and the disruption and damage caused by the 99.9 per cent of insecticides and fungicides that miss their target. Now I was eating organically for my own health.

Did you know that it's almost impossible to wash or peel off all chemicals from your food? This is because some chemicals are contact based, meaning that they kill everything they come into contact with directly, while others are systemic, meaning that they are absorbed by the roots, leaves and all parts of the crop. This is obviously bad not only for the insects, wildlife, people and soil that come into contact with the plant but, because of soil run-off and the fact that the nectar and pollen are affected, also areas for miles around via waterways and insects. It's more tempting for farmers to use systemic chemicals as insects not in contact with the parts of the plant that are sprayed with contact chemicals (for example, hiding in the leaf folds or not yet arrived) are unaffected.

As Guy Watson from Riverford (organic) Farm says, "There is no safe pesticide; as their power comes from disrupting fundamental life processes, there are only degrees of risk" (Watson, n.d.).

Intuitive herbalism

I was overjoyed when Nathaniel wrote to me later in 2017 telling me that I had a place on the Foundation Year in Intuitive Herbalism.

It started in February and we met, a group of eight of us plus Nathaniel, every couple of months for four days. We met a few plants each time, getting to know them through direct experience rather than through books and theoretical knowledge. One of the group was a herbalist and had learned the modern way of classifying plants, learning their Latin names and "known" properties, and had found this unfulfilling. She had wanted to come to know plants properly.

Indeed, there used to be a school in Scotland – the Scottish School of Herbal Medicine – which taught students in just this way, by having them go out and meet the plant before learning about it in the classroom. It has sadly changed now and students might taste as many as 12 herbs in one morning and never actually have proper meetings with them, so it's impossible to go to any depth. When Nathaniel (personal communication) was a student there he reports that:

> We studied around 150 plants, all of which we met as dried herbs and about half as a tea to taste, generally with about 30 minutes to spend on each. We would study 12 each weekend block and giving somewhere around half a day to a day of the weekend to cover these 12.
>
> I only recall doing a more full Goethian plant study (i.e. working with a living plant over a whole day) with Elder and Lady's Mantle and both were semi-optional parts of the summer school – one with Margaret Colquhoun and one with Cas who was in my year and was doing her dissertation on Lady's Mantle.

I've learned from Nathaniel that you only need to know around 12 plants intimately (and you can only get to know around two or three each year this well) to be an effective herbalist. Each plant will reveal its healing powers to you if you develop a genuine, respectful relationship with it. I've done quite a bit of work with him and my cohort of plant friends and humans now, and I know there is far more to learn. But it's not from books – with the exception of Nathaniel's excellent *Weeds in the Heart* (Hughes & Owen, 2018); it's through developing my intuition and a phenomenological ways of seeing the world, a process that started at Schumacher College. Nathaniel teaches that, when treating another person,

> The process of developing skilfulness with intuitive awareness starts with presuming that everything you perceive is a reflection of *you*. Only by knowing your *own* inner/dream landscapes in detail can you start to be reliably aware of the effect on *you* that another person has.

He gave us all a handout on "Experiences of vision and spontaneous knowing", which included the following, grouped under three areas of self: Seer, Empath and Healer.

SEER
- Flashes of insight
- Images and "aha" moments
- Quality of shadow over parts of body
- Sense of other presences in room
- Past/future imagery
- Phrases or words

EMPATH
- Atmosphere
- Frustrated anger/sadness/fear
- Heaviness
- Armour
- Warmth/cold
- Texture – soft/jagged

HEALER
- Tightening belly/shoulders/breath/jaw
- Hunger/thirst
- Intense fatigue
- Yawning
- Softening/hardening
- Crying/spontaneous laughing
- Stopping breathing

I continue to have individual sessions with Nathaniel near Stroud, and often go and visit my father in nearby Bath. Nathaniel has become a friend, along with all the Foundation Year participants with whom I have a WhatsApp group so we are regularly in contact.

Acupuncture – Dr Li Zhang

As mentioned earlier, when I thought I had depression I started building up a team of supporters, professionals who I could go to for relief of depression. One of these was a wonderful Chinese woman, an acupuncturist by the name of Dr Li Zhang, who worked on Mill Road in Cambridge, just at the bottom of our street. I could walk there. It was one of my questions to Adel Helmy before the operation – "How long before I can have acupuncture on my head?" Little did I know then that I wouldn't be getting out of hospital until way after the recommended time.

Li was an amazing support to me when I was allowed home on weekends. She gave me treatments, massaging my head and telling me I would be okay. I really believed her, she said it with such confidence. "You will be okay ... in the medical way", she would say, alluding to the difference between Western and Chinese medicine.

Exercise

From the earliest days of being allowed out of the hospital on weekend leave I was cycling (despite the warnings from Dr Kirker), doing Pilates at the local gym, and restorative yoga classes just up the road from me. During radiotherapy I took up Feldenkrais, a practice I'd read about, which does all sorts of things including connecting the body and brain. I practised with a brilliant local trainer called Jon Nicholson, who has a gym called The Original Gym, based on natural movement. These sessions were sometimes joined by visitors. I also had personal training sessions from Jon where we went to the local park and practised the climbing wall, running and balancing, sometimes with Mike, sometimes separately. I found Jon to be a super-committed, talented, intelligent and kind guy.

Later I took up more cardio-based exercise with stronger yoga classes and BMF (British Military Fitness, now renamed Be Military Fit) in the local park. I continued with BMF until I moved to London where I attended a couple of classes but then, to my shame, I dropped it. I wish I could say there was a good reason for this, but the truth is I just couldn't be bothered to get up early (the classes local to me now are at 7.30 a.m., whereas in Cambridge they had been in the early evenings and late on Saturday mornings). I was usually up that early anyway but doing things. I still do a lot of yoga, though, and love it.

Later still while at OZC, I took a one-day cycle proficiency course on one of my days off, led by a company called Outspoken in Cambridge, which helped me feel more comfortable on the roads. I still cycle in London now though am still not confident enough to cycle in rush hour and tend to ride for pleasure, mainly along the canal.

EMDR (Eye Movement Desensitisation and Reprocessing) – Catherine Smart

I read about this in one of Norman Doidge's books (2016) and then bought a book just on EMDR (Eye Movement Desensitisation and Reprocessing). It's a technique for healing trauma through the body that centres on Rapid Eye Movement, which happens naturally during sleep. Traditionally, the practitioner waves his or her hand or fingers quite fast in front of your face and you have to follow it/them with your eyes, not moving your head. I found one practitioner with whom I had a couple of sessions, but I found the physical journey out to him to be too long and the process unsatisfying, so I found another – Catherine Smart – closer to me and with whom I felt I could relate much more easily. She was great and helped me articulate what it was that was troubling me. She also had an alternative to waving her fingers in front of my face, which I found distracting, preferring to close my eyes, which was a way of tapping into the healing. I would sit facing her with my hands on a cushion and she would literally tap on my hands. I don't know how it worked but it did.

Although I didn't feel like I had much trauma remaining from the experience of brain cancer and all that time in the hospital and rehabilitation centres, I was interested in exploring the technique as it seemed like a short route to healing more deeply entrenched traumas. I had long been aware of a feeling of not being good enough and thought I could use this technique to identify a root for and heal this part of myself. I explored this and other issues with Catherine in weekly sessions over the course of a couple of months and found it largely beneficial.

NSA (Network Spinal Analysis) – Dr Gethin Gray and Dr Fiona Marsden

This is a sort of chiropractic technique that listens to your body and makes adjustments, with very gentle and precise contacts along the spine that help the body to heal emotional and physical damage and imbalances. Here's what one NSA practitioner (Shiozawa, n.d.) has to say about it:

> NSA utilises very gentle (no "cracking") specific contacts along the spine, allowing the brain to respond causing it to find embedded tension within the central nervous system, primarily in the spinal cord. When the brain and spinal cord can find and connect to those tensions, the body will respond by doing a series of breaths or movements which ultimately cause that tension to be released. Each adjustment is referred to more specifically as an "entrainment" because they allow the brain and nervous system to learn and build inner strategies for better mobility, more breath, and more ease inside the body.

My recent experience of NSA has been with two practitioners, and in fact it was first recommended as a technique by my chiropractor, Liz, shortly before she moved to the US. I looked it up and found a practitioner in

London (there weren't any in Cambridge at that time) and started going to him (Dr Gethin Gray). That first session with Gethin in the summer of 2017 was amazing. I was still at the stage of finding certain music off-putting and asked him to turn down the music when it came to a song with lyrics. He was very obliging and really seemed to understand. Not only that but he was willing to massage my bald head, which I really craved (it was shortly after radiotherapy).

My dad then recommended a chiropractor in London called Dr Fiona Marsden, whom his chiropractor in Bath had recommended when he talked about me. He'd said that if Dr Elizabeth Lim (our previous chiropractor) was a white witch – as we used to call her – Dr Thomasina Craster was a sorceress and had helped with his spine immeasurably. He didn't know that Thomasina was an NSA practitioner, so when I went to see Fiona I asked her what she did. I was surprised to see two other beds in the room and even more surprised when I understood that she was going to be delivering care to three of us at the same time. She assumed I'd been under Thomasina's care and would therefore have known what she did as I been recommended by Thomasina (I had booked an appointment with Thomasina but hadn't actually met her by that point).

When I saw these three beds I was reminded of a session I'd had at a centre in Totnes, while at Schumacher College. It was the very same technique! I don't remember much about the one in Totnes except that it was done in a group, and at the time I moved a lot (it was just after the Body and Earth course so I was used to moving) and made a lot of noise. I am now seeing both Gethin and Fiona (who both know *of* each other and actually *know* each other, as practitioners in the small world of NSA tend to) and finding it really beneficial. I can't explain it exactly but I feel more confident, clearer and stronger in my body and voice. Others have noticed too, especially those who can see energy and auras.

Yoga nidra

Yoga nidra is a state of consciousness between waking and sleeping, like the "going to sleep" stage. It is a state in which the body is completely relaxed, and the practitioner becomes systematically and increasingly aware of the inner world by following a set of verbal instructions. My friend, Jane, had put me onto it before the diagnosis – she had practised and taught it for years. Here's what she has to say about it:

> This simple practice helps us to let go of muscular tension, and teaches us how to release fears, anxieties, phobias and trauma. It is

totally safe, environmentally friendly, drug and cost free, and almost anyone, regardless of age, can learn how to do it. Regular practice can be both curative and preventative.

(Classical Yoga, n.d.)

I didn't do it right away but as soon as I got the diagnosis I started practising it in preparation for the recovery period. It has a part in it that says: "Be aware of stillness throughout your whole body. 'I can move my body but I'm choosing to not move my body' ", which I thought would be useful if the worst happened and I did end up with SMA Syndrome.

As it was, it wasn't at all useful as I thought the iPod recording was corrupted and full of subliminal messages telling me to masturbate – I was very suspicious of Apple as a company. There's a part in the recording which says, "Be aware of the abdomen: explore what is there" that I thought was implying "explore your genitals". I said this to Mike, who didn't believe me, so I also said it to my sister Debs and asked her to convince him. She didn't believe me either – because it wasn't true! – but she hid this from me, and Mike dutifully brought the actual CD in and a machine to play it on (he had to borrow one from my niece, Hannah).

Hyperbaric Oxygen Therapy (HBO)

I started to have sessions of HBO on the advice of my naturopath, in early 2019. It is a way of getting oxygen into the cells, essential for all cell functions and especially when fighting diseases and conditions such as cancer. I had them mostly at a multiple sclerosis centre in Walthamstow. It is often used after radiotherapy.

It is well known that most cancer cells do not like oxygen. Most tumours have blood supplies that leave parts of the tumour starved of oxygen, or "hypoxic", making them resistant to radiotherapy. The vessels are also leaky, stopping chemotherapy drugs penetrating deeply enough to kill the growth. This means that tumours well supplied with oxygen are actually more vulnerable.

Hyperbaric oxygen was first used 60 years ago to increase cellular oxygen delivery and thus overcome hypoxia as a cause of tumour radioresistance. This scientifically proven application of hyperbaric oxygen is now unused.

(Coles, Williams & Burnet, 1999: 1076)

The experience has been interesting and I've now had the first 20 sessions at 16 feet (which is roughly equivalent to 50 kilopascals – kPa, or 0.5 atmospheres – ATM). Some of these were in a diving bell with room for six people where we all sat up in chairs with oxygen masks on, and others were in a solo chamber, lying down with a nasal canula. It was more comfortable lying down as I could meditate and it was much closer, but it was also slightly drying on the nostrils and more expensive. I continued with the solo chamber for a few more weeks and will continue with it for a while longer. There's no way of testing whether the oxygen is having an effect and I didn't actually feel any different until it was taken up to 100 kPa (1 ATM or 32 feet) – since then I've felt like I'm walking on air after most sessions!

Love and support

Friends as well as family did so many amazing things for me. Tabitha (Tab), one of my most creative friends, brought in small homemade cards in an envelope while I was on the A ward at Addenbrooke's, each with a particular happy memory on it so that I could choose one at random and dwell on it while I was alone. She brought in bunting with the words "Get Well Jelly", which she offered to let me help her put together. She didn't actually intend it and was apologetic when I later told her, but the fiddliness of threading the ribbon through the pieces of bunting was great for my fine motor co-ordination.

She made me another for my birthday that year saying "Well Jel" – this was after a poem my father had obtained from my favourite living poet, Matt Harvey, a Totnes poet to whom Jane had first introduced me years before and who I'd met in Totnes. He's a great performance poet but his poems bear reading by themselves too, and I read quite a few of them to my classmates at Schumacher at morning meetings over the year. They always had people either in fits of laughter or tears. My father had seen Matt's book, *The Hole in the Sum of My Parts* (2005) in my hospital room (brought in at my request to help me develop my speaking voice) and asked to borrow it for the train ride home. I said yes, of course, as long as he promised to return it or buy me another as it was precious to me. He went one step further and contacted Matt, telling him I was a fan and what I was going through. Matt then went one step further again by sending my father another copy of the book, not only signed but with an extra poem in it, handwritten especially for me (Figure 8.3).

Sal, another friend who I've mentioned earlier, was also a star, supporting me from the "depression" onwards. She said, when she found out

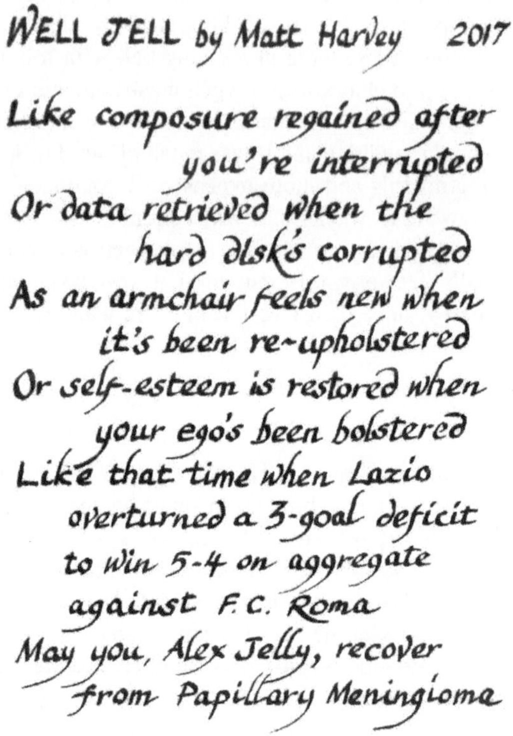

WELL JELL by Matt Harvey   2017

Like composure regained after
         you're interrupted
Or data retrieved when the
      hard disk's corrupted
As an armchair feels new when
      it's been re-upholstered
Or self-esteem is restored when
      your ego's been bolstered
Like that time when Lazio
   overturned a 3-goal deficit
   to win 5-4 on aggregate
   against F.C. Roma
May you, Alex Jelly, recover
      from Papillary Meningioma

Figure 8.3 Calligraphed version of the Matt Harvey poem.

about the tumour, "At least we know what we're dealing with now" and it was that "we" that was important because it let me know I wasn't alone. She was a wonderful practical help later when I moved onto the naturopathy plan and had huge numbers of supplements to deal with, setting up spreadsheets, ordering more when it was time to, setting up repeat prescriptions for my pharmaceutical drugs, and coming all the way from near Manchester almost every week. It must have been a long and expensive journey and she wasn't in salaried employment at the time, but she never complained or even mentioned it. It was only months afterwards that I realised what a big deal that was.

Becs is another friend from the same group – we were all at school together. She was living in South Africa at the time of the tumour but flew all the way back for a few days to see me! And Melanie (Mela) too; she's so busy with her three wonderful children and full-time job as a GP, but she made time to come and see me at least twice in the hospital. They were all so amazing. Katie and Mark, who I mention elsewhere, were great too. Malc is another friend who I re-made contact with after a few months of not seeing him, when I thought I had depression. He's always been there for me and this time was no exception. Both our birthdays are in July and we're the same age, so we had a joint thirtieth birthday party and a joint fortieth birthday party and we fully intend to have a joint fiftieth. He came to see me in hospital several times and he's a great conversationalist so I sometimes had to take breaks and he was always fine with it. He was the one who brought in noses for Red Nose Day.

Lynn is another friend who's been through some tough times in recent years, having to say goodbye to her mother who passed away. Her mother had vascular dementia and was in a care home so it was really hard for her. She certainly wasn't fazed by the hospital environment. She's the most wonderful baker, even more so now as she is (at the time of writing) working in a bakery called Flour, Water and Salt, near Macclesfield, having completed a year-long Advanced Diploma in Baking at the School of Artisan Food. She used to bring me cake which, to be honest, I found too dry (as I found most food), but it was good to have something truly delicious to offer other guests and I used to enjoy tiny pieces.

Yumi is a friend I found through massage. She's a wonderful masseur and healer and came to visit me quite early on in hospital – I think Mike invited her thinking she would give me a healing session, but she gave me far more than that. It was in the days before I was able to speak. As we sat there, she first told me she was sure I would be okay, as I'd been a friend to so many people and plants. Then she said she'd been walking in Mill Road Cemetery, a place where I'd been many times and recently with her, and could feel my energy there. This meant a lot to me as I loved it there. I had in my head that we'd met before we lived in Cambridge as Tab (who always remembered things for me: I used to call her "my memory") had said to me that I'd emailed her from India where I did my Reiki training and spoke of a woman named Yumi. I didn't remember this myself and would swear that I hadn't met her on the Reiki course, but hadn't had a chance to check this out with her and now couldn't speak!

Yumi somehow knew I had something to tell her and stopped talking. We just stared into each other's eyes for the longest time. It was beautiful and very soulful and better than any words and I felt we'd definitely met before. It must have been in another lifetime though. When I could speak I met up with Yumi in Cambridge. We went for a post-massage meditation under a yew tree and I spoke to her of this. We worked out that even though we definitely hadn't been on the same course at the same time, we'd both been attuned by the same teacher in the same remote village, and possibly even in the same year! But on top of this we both feel we've met before in some past life.

Francine and Tareq

Francine is another friend from school – in the same group as Sal, Tab, Becs and Mela. She works for the UN and was about to move to Delhi to head up UNDP at the time of my operation. She came back to see her family and friends in the summer of 2017 though and made the trip to the BIRT in Ely to see me, first with her husband, Tareq, and then a second time alone. I had been to their wedding in Jerusalem years before and am very fond of Tareq. Her visit coincided with one from my dad, who had come with me to see them in Jordan years before. The woman who was at the time looking after their children (as Francine and Tareq were away at work during the day) had called Dad "Sir Bruce" and it caught on. My dad recalled that when Tareq met him at the entrance to the BIRT and called him "Sir Bruce", you should have seen the look on the staff's faces as they wondered whether this man was really a knight of the realm! Francine, Tareq, my dad and Mike and I all went out for dinner in our (by now favourite) restaurant in Ely.

Francine came again a few days before they were due to leave the UK and interviewed me for parts of this book. At the time she was just helping me to write stories that I didn't want to forget, but they were so useful for this book. She had studied Anthropology at Cambridge and is a published author so it was really helpful, not to mention loving. I remember crying a lot, as I did at that time. She's lovely and a great friend.

The Annas

I've got two lovely friends called Anna. Annas are always nice. That's the rule. They have to be; they can't help it. And they have to make things, delicious things. Both my Annas did for me. Anna 1 as I'll call her, brought me nice-smelling things from Sussex as if she'd been given a hint – which she hadn't – that my sense of smell was the first to return. She also brought foraged birch-sap water, which just happened to be the perfect drink for me for reasons that I won't go into here. She also brought me some scented wash things, either homemade or from Neal's Yard, and a bergamot, which tastes like a cross between a tangerine and a lemon with a slight Earl Grey flavour. I do know that I immediately bit into it, skin and all, excited by the deliciousness of it. Mike took it away from me, thinking I'd mistaken it for something, but I hadn't – I was just enamoured of the citrusy flavour and knew it would be taken away soon by one of the nurses.

Anna 2 came to see me early on. She's a friend from Cambridge who I knew through Mike but we had become friends during my "depression" and been for lots of walks and talks and I found her to be a good confidante. She was doing a counselling course but never tried to counsel me. She had recommended her (and now my) homeopath, Marlow, for which I'm eternally grateful. Anna used to be heavily involved in the Transition movement – that's the kind of person she is, always giving and organising. She's also great at DIY, making kombucha and making me laugh. When she came to visit I gave her a hand massage, which I think she liked. I just wanted to use my hands. She's one of my soul sisters. We've been friends for a couple of years now, and she started an informal, then increasingly formal, singing group which still meets every couple of weeks in Cambridge. Recently, I went with her to Voicecamp, a week-long camping and singing event. When I was at the BIRT, Anna came and sang with and to me in my room. She has the most beautiful voice and I wanted to get her on the programme for other patients – even if they couldn't sing they could bathe in the sound. Unfortunately, the BIRT never took this up. I did, however, send a recording I'd made of the two of us singing a one-line song, Shalom, to Mike's dad.

I've already mentioned my friends, Emilie and Evandro, who used to make visits all the way from South London to Cambridge, on a couple of occasions even getting to the hospital only to be told I was too tired for visitors. Who knows who else I turned down at the last minute? They also came to see me when I went home for the weekend – on one memorable occasion we were sitting in the garden when I explained that I was finding eye contact difficult and went inside for a straw hat which I wore to cover my eyes. Emilie joined me in comedy/sympathy and I've got a wonderful photo of us both wearing our scarves over our eyes (Figure 8.4).

Similarly, on my birthday, when I didn't want to plan anything, Mike stepped in and sent an invite to some of my best friends, including my two sisters, all of whom dutifully turned up. We had a garden party and everyone brought food. Debs played a starring role, bringing a raw lasagne and sushi with sunflower-seed "rice" and Cat did all the washing up. Again, I couldn't make eye contact and wore sunglasses. I couldn't bear crowds either. It was also in the early days of taking cannabis oil so I was completely stoned. It was a hot day so everyone was sitting around the garden table under an umbrella and later I went round the table just holding hands with each person and talking to them – or doing more

Figure 8.4 Emilie and I – can't see each other!

listening than talking in fact – and they were all wonderfully under-standing. I even went up for a siesta at one stage while my guests enter-tained each other. *And* they didn't outstay their welcome. Tab made me a folder of poetry contributions from most of my friends, including the more distant ones who didn't come to see me in hospital but who I always knew were there in the background, rooting for me. My dad gave me the Matt Harvey poem, the calligraphed version that I've mentioned earlier. So despite my protests it was a good birthday and I felt really loved.

Childhood friends like Claire and Bron came to visit regularly too, although Bron was away in South Africa for the first few weeks and Claire lives in Portishead so couldn't come that often. But when each of them did it was great.

Tab used to come over and read to me in the sunshine of the garden, once bringing a book I'd given her as a present years ago. It's called Star Girl and is about an American home-schooled girl joining a high school. She's magical and independent and generous and it is the sweetest story. Tab used to read parts of it to me while I was lying in the shade and she was sitting in the sun (it has always been this way with us, both of us loving being outside but she loving direct sunshine rather more than me). One day as she was reading, she happened to look up and see a smiley face in the sky, drawn by a plane right above us. She pointed to it and took a photo to post on the WhatsApp update group. It was a sign to both of us that everything would be okay. We didn't manage to finish the book together but she recorded herself reading the last chapter and sent it to me! I love her voice and her care.

Ola, Boris and Bar

My neighbours, Ola and Boris, were two of my most committed visitors as they lived in Cambridge. They were, in fact, the first of our neighbours that we met and we've always been great friends. Ola is an artist and published author. When she saw me colouring in she offered to lend me her studio and art materials when I got out of hospital. She also brought me food, and later I found out that she'd frequently dropped off food for Mike or invited him round after long days at the hospital. Boris was great too – he's not much of a talker but just sat there and held my hand. I think I quite often was too tired to see them but they never minded.

Their daughter, Bar, is a dancer. One sunny afternoon Ola brought her to visit me. We were all outside in the Jubilee Gardens and I wanted to re-learn how to jump. I just couldn't leave the ground and really wanted to. As I stood there on the grass, adopting the plié position and finally – for the first time in months – jumping into the air, holding both their hands at first – I felt such joy, such elation in such a simple act!

Friends from afar

David, one of my great friends from school, was away on a trip to India when I had the operation, but he kept sending packages of Indian clothes – which I wore, much to the interest of Indian staff and the amusement of others – and videos from his trip (Figure 8.5).

One day I overheard a patient's husband telling her a joke that ended with someone saying something in a funny accent. I somehow got scared that a particular video David sent me from India would end in the same line and that this would mean he would die – I didn't want to watch it to the end and made Mike take it away! This, combined with the fact that he was travelling in almost exactly the same remote area of India I had been in when I contracted my urine infection and that the patient who used to shout out names at night once shouted David's name, made me petrified for his safety.

He also sent postcards when he was back in the UK, with an app that allows you to make up postcards with your own photos and messages and sends them for you. He sent the most beautiful shot (his own photo) of dolphins leaping out of the water around the Isle of Skye with the message "Do you feel like this dolphin – exuberant?"

Figure 8.5 Me in Indian gear sent by my friend, David, unwrapping colourful pillowcases, also from David.

Countless examples abound of love shown to me by friends and family. From Mike tucking me in at night – he developed this way of arranging my blankets so that I could pull them around me when it got cold and put a pillow at my feet to prop my feet up, speaking to the nurses to extend visiting hours, and coming with me every day to radiotherapy – to my sister Debs coming over from Sussex to Cambridge for two days each week, cooking, cleaning our house and keeping Mike company – to all the cards and letters of support from random people as well as close friends and family. I couldn't have got through it without them all.

My two – no, three, no, wait, make that four – seizures

My first seizure was directly after the operation. The first I knew of it was when I questioned why I was on anti-seizure medication a couple of months or so later, at Addenbrooke's. Neither Mike nor I knew about it and it's quite common so none of the medical staff had mentioned it to us specifically. Mike had got hold of my medical notes, but neither he nor I had gone through them: I wasn't ready to read at that point and he had more important things on his mind.

The second was in June 2017 when I unilaterally came off the Keppra (anti-seizure medication) while at the BIRT. I would go home at weekends and had already successfully come off the medication for two weekends in a row. At the end of the third weekend, as Mike and I were driving back, we were having a heated conversation about radiotherapy, which I had yet to make my mind up about. Mike thought I should have it. I started fitting and he had to do several things at the same time: work out what was happening to me and how to help (amazingly no one from Addenbrooke's or the BIRT had thought to warn us that it might happen or advise Mike what to do in the event); try to pull off the road and park somewhere safely; call an ambulance. Impressively, he had the presence of mind to do all three (he also gave me CPR, which we found out later was unnecessary, but how was he to know?)

The third was in April 2018 when I was reducing the medication gradually, post-radiotherapy, this time in line with – and even rather more conservatively than – my neuro-oncologist had agreed. Mike and I were in the bath together on a Sunday night, totally calm, when it happened. It must have been scary for him, but at least this time he knew what to do. I came to consciousness sitting in very little bath water as he had drained it – another act of impressive thinking – and he helped me out of the bath and helped me into bed. He messaged my family first to let them know and, of course, they were so thankful that he had been there for me.

I couldn't remember anything about the seizure or how it had happened so he had to describe it to me. He said I just started hanging my head to one side and fitting with no warning or obvious signs beforehand. He made me promise not to get out of bed in the night without waking him up. I had to get up to use the bathroom as I had drunk so much water after the seizure so I did have to wake him up and he was brilliant about it, guiding me to the bathroom, waiting for me, and then guiding me back to bed. He never once complained or made me feel bad. Only later did he confess that he'd been really traumatised by it.

The fourth was at the end of March 2019 when I had run out of Keppra and for various reasons (none of them my fault) couldn't get hold of any more. I had just come back from Spain by train and had a long and stressful journey home, getting back at around 2 a.m. on the Saturday morning. I was then at a yoga class later that morning and on my way up from a downward dog pose, stumbled, fell and had a seizure, only coming round to an empty room and an ambulance on its way. As usual, I didn't remember anything about it and there had been no warning signs. As I'd so recently had a perfectly clear brain scan, I didn't need to stay in hospital for a scan and only stayed for an hour or so for the usual blood pressure and blood tests. Tab was her usual star self, coming to see me and picking up the repeat prescription the next day, and my sister Cat heroically came to collect me as I was going to hers anyway for Mothers' Day the following day. I had been planning to come off the medication but now I know I can't, at least not for a while.

Chapter 9

Life today

Alex Jelly

Life today is good. I still have brain scans every three months, still regularly see my neuro-oncologist, naturopath, and homeopath, NET practitioners and herbalist, and go for occasional sessions with my acupuncturist in Cambridge. I've recently moved into a beautiful flat in London and the light and the garden there make me very happy. The writing of this book has progressed successfully and served me well.

My most recent scan at the time of writing also included a DTI (Diffusion Tensor Imagery) or DT-MRI. My neuro-oncologist commented during the follow-up meeting that while this was his area of interest he hadn't actually ordered it so I don't know why I had it, but it showed the direction of connections in the brain. He said in his follow-up letter that "It was interesting to observe the intact white matter in the frontal lobes, despite ... surgery and radiation therapy."

I've joined a local Unionist church, a non-religious version, so it has all the community, singing and readings of any other church except they're all non-religious, mostly drawn from literature, with a different theme each quarter. "We believe in Good" is the slogan! It's a "radically inclusive" community and based on a history of dissent and striving for social justice. Mary Wollstonecraft, grandmother of the feminist movement, is celebrated there as she lived on nearby Newington Green.

I'm cycling, doing yoga and occasional Be Military Fitness sessions in my local park. I'm reading lots of good books and can now watch films and listen to loud music (and so go to gigs and the cinema) as I have been able to for some time now. I also go semi-regularly to the theatre and to dance shows. I've started a Women's Group at the church and co-facilitate it with a lovely woman from the same community.

As of March 2019, I am training as a facilitator for Rites for Girls, a newish organisation set up by Kim McCabe, author of the bestselling book *From Daughter to Woman*. It's facilitation for groups of young girls to prevent the trauma that's often experienced as part of puberty. I hope to be qualified by the end of next year, having facilitated my first group of girls for a full 12-month period.

Mike and I are still friends; I see my friends and family regularly and am sociable and enjoying the culture and wild spaces of London. I was interested in starting a second year of Intuitive Herbalism when Nathaniel offered it in the future, but have now decided it would be taking on too much; I am generally busy, healthy and enjoying life. I feel like I've made the transformation into the person I'm meant to be (for now – we're all constantly changing) and loving it.

I did a sponsored 10km walk through Windsor for The Brain Tumour Charity in October 2018, and together with my older sister Cat raised over 10 per cent of the total raised by everyone who took part (£5000 not including Gift Aid). One of the things this did was reconnect me to old friends, in particular one from university – Bev – who's still got as big a heart as he did at university. We email each other regularly and plan to meet soon when he's down in London.

I don't want to tempt fate but I'm living proof that one can go through SMA Syndrome, psychosis and rare, aggressive brain cancer and not only survive but have a normal life again.

Part II

Background information from Adel Helmy and Barbara A. Wilson

Chapter 10

Meningioma and the brain

Adel Helmy

The human brain is the most complex structure in the known universe: understanding this organ is the challenge that faces modern neuroscience. The brain controls every aspect of our bodily function, from movements to our senses and to our sense of identity. This diversity means that abnormalities that affect the brain, like brain tumours, can present in many different ways depending on which parts of the brain they affect.

Brain tumours are classified by the World Health Organization (WHO) based on the cell types within the tumour, how quickly the cells divide, and in some cases, the genetic abnormalities in the tumour cells. In the most recent classification system (WHO, 2016) there are over 100 different subtypes. This makes it difficult to generalise about brain tumours. In this chapter, we will talk specifically about one type of brain tumour, meningioma. In the WHO classification, although there are many subtypes described, there are three categories called "grades" that occur. The grade reflects the aggressiveness of the cells within the tumour, which relates to the risk of the tumour growing quickly and the chance of it growing back again after being removed. Grade 1 (70–80 per cent) is the slowest growing and least aggressive type. Grade 2 (20–30 per cent), also called atypical meningioma, is intermediate and is increasingly diagnosed, not because meningiomas have changed but because the WHO classification has changed. Grade 3 (1–2 per cent), sometimes called anaplastic or malignant meningioma, are the most aggressive type and require the most aggressive treatments. This rarest subtype is the form that Alex suffered from.

Meningiomas account for about one-third of all tumours in the skull. Meningiomas are not strictly tumours of the brain, as they arise from the lining of the brain and spine – the *meninges*. A specific type of cell in the lining of the brain, called the arachnoid cap cell, forms these tumours when it grows uncontrollably. Meningiomas of the head are more common in women than men (2:1) and are commonest in late middle age, although they can occur at any age and in either sex. Meningiomas are sometimes described as "benign" tumours, however the word benign is not a good description. Meningiomas are rarely malignant or cancerous in the sense that they can spread outside the brain to other organs, such as the lung or liver. Nevertheless, they can cause severe neurological problems and can be a risk to a person's life. Similarly, for some types of meningioma, the treatment required is anything but benign.

What causes meningiomas?

Like all tumours, the underlying cause of meningioma is a genetic abnormality that causes the cells within the tumour to grow in an uncontrolled fashion. The underlying reason for the genetic abnormality is not known in the majority of cases. These are called *sporadic* tumours and are not hereditary. Rarely, some tumour syndromes can run in families. For example, neurofibromatosis type 2 (NF2) commonly results in meningioma formation. Nevertheless, syndromes like NF2 (one in 60,000 people) are in themselves rare so most meningiomas are still sporadic.

Radiation therapy to the brain is known to cause meningiomas. Typically, this is related to people who had malignant brain tumours as young children. This is because the *latency* – the time between having radiation and getting a tumour – can be several decades, and because childhood malignant brain tumours often need large doses of radiation. As with all brain tumours, mobile phone use is not related to meningioma formation.

Meningiomas have receptors on their cells that respond to progesterone and this may be the reason they are more common in women. Meningiomas can also grow more rapidly or swell during pregnancy, but the fact that they also occur in men suggests that hormonal factors are not involved in causing the tumour in the first place.

How do meningiomas cause symptoms?

Meningiomas can affect any part of the brain or spine. Brain tumours, in general, can present in one of four ways. First, they can affect a part of the brain that has a specific function and cause a problem with that function. Medically, we call this a *focal neurological deficit*. For example, if a tumour presses on the nerve to the eye it can cause blurring or loss of vision. If it presses on the language part of the brain it can cause speech or writing problems. Sometimes these neurological deficits can be quite subtle and as the tumours can grow slowly the symptoms may come on over months or years and can be difficult to spot at first. For example, compression of the frontal lobes can cause personality changes and *abulia* – a loss of desire to do things. These tumours are notorious for being diagnosed late as the symptoms may mimic commoner diseases such as depression.

Second, meningiomas can also present with *seizures*. A seizure is uncontrolled electrical activity in the brain. Nerve cells use electrical impulses to communicate with each other and carry out the complex processing that occurs in the brain. When this electrical activity is uncontrolled, the portion of the brain affected stops functioning. Seizures can affect one part of the brain, called *partial seizures*, or the whole of the brain, called *generalised seizures*. Partial seizures can cause a wide range of symptoms, similar to the focal neurological deficits described above. Generalised seizures cause the individual to lose consciousness, although the distinction is not always clear cut as partial seizures can start in one place and then spread throughout the whole brain (*partial seizures with secondary generalisation*). The wide variety of patterns of seizures can sometimes make them difficult to spot and diagnose. Seizures are usually treated in their own right with anti-seizure drugs, separate to the treatment options described below.

Third, any tumour in the head can present with *raised pressure in the head*. This raised pressure can cause headaches, but the headaches tend to have certain characteristics. The headache is worse on lying flat, bending forwards or coughing and straining. It tends to come on in the morning and may resolve during the day. It can also be associated with nausea and vomiting and blurred vision. Headache is such a common symptom that it is important to realise that most headaches do not have these features and have nothing to do with brain tumours. The headaches associated with brain tumours don't tend to come and go from day to day as the tumour is always there: if a brain tumour is the cause the headaches occur more and more frequently as time goes on.

Fourth, brain tumours can present with disturbances of pituitary hormones. This is a very rare way for meningiomas to present, although it is a common way for pituitary tumours to come to light.

How are meningiomas treated?

Meningioma is usually a slow-growing tumour and small tumours may cause no problems at all. With the increase in the availability and use of sensitive brain scanners, small asymptomatic meningiomas are being discovered far more frequently. This discovery can often cause a number of problems for patients and doctors. Being told that you have a "brain tumour" is a traumatic event that causes understandable anxiety. Even if people are reassured that the scan shows a likely meningioma, the knowledge that "something is there" can significantly impact a person's quality of life. Symptoms that may have been dismissed as trivial or which are unlikely to relate to the meningioma can take on a debilitating nature and stop people enjoying their lives as they previously did.

From the medical perspective, if a small meningioma is found on a scan while looking for something else (*incidentally*), the question arises as to what to do about it. The majority of these patients are followed up with *active surveillance*, that is to say they have scans from time to time to keep an eye on the tumour. If the tumour is stable or slowly growing, they may never need any other treatment. If the tumour grows or causes symptoms, then other treatments can be considered. The gap or interval between scans can be difficult to judge. If the scans are too closely spaced, then they are less likely to demonstrate tumour growth, they use up a lot of hospital resource and they cause more anxiety and disruption to people's lives. If they are spaced out too far, there may be a concern that the tumour grows substantially between scans. In general, active surveillance for meningioma involves scans that are many months or years apart. Active surveillance is the commonest management plan for meningiomas.

Radiotherapy is the use of some types of (ionising) radiation to damage a tumour to stop it growing. Radiotherapy is a very effective treatment, particularly for small tumours because the dose needed is smaller. It is also very useful for tumours that are in locations where a tumour cannot be removed because of damage to surrounding structures (like important nerves and arteries) that are within, or closely related to, the tumour. The skill in delivering radiation treatment is in maximising the dose to the tumour while minimising the damage to the normal brain structures. This is done in several ways. Multiple beams of radiation can be used to concentrate the radiation on a target while the surrounding tissue only gets a tiny fraction of this dose. Second, the treatments can be broken up into several visits, *fractionation*, to give time for the normal tissues to recover before focusing the radiation on the tumour once more.

Radiation also has an important role in reducing the chances of a tumour growing back after it has been removed at surgery. This is called *adjuvant* radiotherapy, and is recommended for grade 3 meningiomas because they have a higher chance of growing back. For grade 2 meningiomas, it is not clear whether they should have radiotherapy straight after having an operation or waiting to see if anything grows back first. This is an area of active study in clinical trials. Grade 1 meningiomas are rarely treated with adjuvant radiotherapy unless they are in an awkward location that prevents further operations.

Neurosurgery is an effective treatment for meningiomas but it is never considered lightly. It is usually reserved for larger tumours and those that press on critical structures in the brain that cause the patient symptoms. Although any tumour can be removed from any part of the brain, there is always a cost to the patient. Even if surgery goes perfectly, patients often develop neurological problems around the time of surgery due to the manipulation of the brain, particularly because the brain surrounding the tumour is already compressed and its function may be disturbed and vulnerable. Often patients will have profound fatigue for many weeks, and sometimes months, after surgery. It is not clear whether this extreme tiredness relates to manipulating the brain, the trauma of surgery or the need for the brain to recover. There are other more mundane, but potentially disruptive effects of surgery: in the UK, there are strict regulations about time off driving after having an operation – typically six months for a grade 1 meningioma, and one year for a grade 2 meningioma.

How is the surgery done?

Neurosurgery for meningiomas is done with a general anaesthetic and usually involves making a cut in the skin and taking out a disc of bone, something called a *craniotomy*. A few unusual locations of meningioma near the roof of the nose can be taken out with an endoscope through the nose, but these are rare approaches. After doing a craniotomy, the key thing in surgery for meningiomas is taking away the blood supply. These are tumours with a lot of blood supply, and during a long operation a lot of blood can be lost, to the extent it can become a risk to the patient's life. Understanding the anatomy of the blood vessels to the meningioma is key in designing how to approach different meningiomas surgically. Often meningiomas will also draw blood from the normal blood vessels in the surrounding brain tissue and this can make the surgery difficult. Normal blood vessels providing blood to the brain must be preserved to avoid causing strokes, while the branches of these blood vessels to the tumour have to be divided to get the tumour out.

Usually meningiomas are removed piecemeal by removing the bulk from within the tumour, called *debulking*, to allow the tumour to collapse in on itself and for the boundary of the tumour with brain tissue to become visible. The tumour can then be gradually peeled away from the surrounding normal tissue, carefully dissecting off any important blood vessels or brain tissue. Some of these important structures are only millimetres in diameter, so a special microscope is used to allow the surgery to be carried out delicately and safely. One of the other factors that makes taking meningiomas out difficult is larger blood vessels and nerves going through the tumour. In this case, debulking the tumour from the inside is potentially very dangerous as it can damage structures that run through the tumour.

Papillary meningioma

Papillary meningioma is one of the rarest and most aggressive type of meningioma, and is grade 3. It is the tumour type that Alex suffered from. These tumours are so aggressive that they are one of the rare types that can spread beyond the brain in 25 per cent of cases. The aggressive nature of these tumours mean that the boundary between tumour and brain is often lost; medically, this is called *brain invasion*. This makes the surgery more difficult and it makes it more likely that the surrounding brain is affected after the surgery.

After surgery for grade 3 tumours, even if there is a complete removal of the tumour, radiotherapy is recommended afterwards to minimise the risk of the tumour returning.

Alex's scans

Figure 10.1 features MRI scans with injected contrast that show the tumour as a bright mass near the centre of the brain. MRI scans are taken as slices through the head. The supplementary motor area is either side of the tumour, and compressed on both sides. This makes the chances of developing Supplementary Motor Area Syndrome much higher.

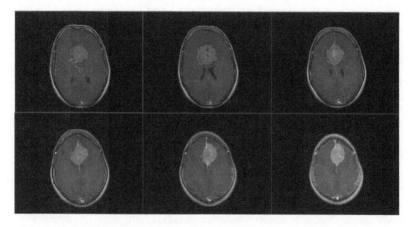

Figure 10.1 Alex's Brain Scans.

Chapter 11

Supplementary Motor Area Syndrome

Adel Helmy

There are only two ways that the brain interacts with the outside world. First, there are our five senses. These provide all the information about the world around us that we perceive. This perception is not perfect, and is tailored to interpreting the world around us. The simple optical illusion in Figure 11.1 demonstrates how the brain often "fills in" information that is not there to allow us to make sense of the world.

The "Penrose triangle" by Escher (1971: see Figure 11.1) is an example of an impossible shape that uses shading to trick our visual system into extracting information about perspective and reconstructing a two-dimensional drawing into a three-dimensional object.

The art of Escher uses these principles to generate much more complex and perplexing images.

Many great philosophers have recognised the limitations of our senses, the implications on how we understand the world around us, and in the most extreme sense, whether the world exists at all. This forms the basis of Rene Descartes' infamous quotation: "je pense, donc je suis; cogito ergo

Figure 11.1 The 'Penrose triangle' by Escher (1971).

sum" [I think therefore I am]. The same ideas are common in popular culture from *The Matrix* to *Inception*: how do we know what is real and what is a trick of the mind?

If we put to one side the larger question as to whether the world we inhabit is real or not, there is certainly only one way we can influence it – movement. Our muscles are the only way that our brains can impact on the world around us. Whether that is by moving objects with our arms, walking with our legs, making facial expressions to convey emotion or tightening our vocal cords while carefully exhaling to make speech, there is no other way. In simple biological terms, our brains have one function – to change sensory perceptions into co-ordinated movements that allow us to perpetuate our species.

The internal monologue of our consciousness is trapped within our brains, unable to communicate with the outside world unless it breaks out through the careful co-ordination of our muscles. All our hopes, dreams and aspirations have no direct bearing on the outside world without the part of the brain responsible for movement – the *motor system*.

How is the motor system of the brain organised?

The motor system of the brain is made up of three main components. The first is the *pyramidal* system. This part of the brain is the nerve cells and fibres that start in the brain (primary motor cortex) and pass down to the spinal cord, and the nerve cells in the spinal cord that connect to the muscles. It is the part of the nervous system that connects the brain with the muscles, but also helps to co-ordinate how groups of muscles work

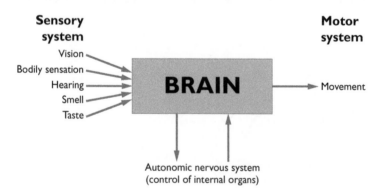

Figure 11.2 How is the brain organised?

together. It is called the pyramidal system because the fibres at the lower part of the brain, called the brainstem, make a pyramid shape. The second part of the motor system is the *cerebellum*, or 'little brain'. It is a structure on the back part of the brain that is involved with co-ordinating muscular movement. The third part of the brain is the *basal ganglia*. These are a group of structures near the middle of the brain that are involved with initiation of movement. The basal ganglia are involved with deciding which movements should go ahead and sending the messages to the pyramidal system to get things started.

The basal ganglia interact with a portion of the brain called the *Supplementary Motor Area* (SMA), which is immediately adjacent to the primary motor cortex. The SMA may have other important functions, but it is clear that the SMA is required to initiate internally generated movements. If recordings are taken in the brain at the time that movements take place then the SMA is activated a few hundred milliseconds before activation is seen in the primary motor cortex.

What is the Supplementary Motor Area Syndrome (SMAS)?

After surgery near the SMA, patients can develop problems with movement, called the SMAS. Typically, this syndrome results in complete paralysis to voluntary movement *(akinesia)* down the opposite side of the body. The complete absence of movement down one side, rather than just weakness, is often a clue as to the presence of SMAS, rather than damage to the pyramidal system. Patients often recover from these symptoms rapidly or suddenly several days to weeks later, although subtle problems can persist for weeks or months. With severe cases, other features such as an inability to speak *(mutism)*, slowing of thought and repeating movements *(perseveration)* can occur. In patients who suffer SMAS, automatic movements such as yawning and swallowing still occur normally; it is only the voluntary movements that are lost.

In Alex's case, she developed a particularly severe SMAS, to the extent that she did not even open her eyes. In the early stages of her post-operative period it was very difficult to diagnose SMAS. The diagnosis was based on several findings: first, the post-operative MRI which did not show any signs of other brain damage; second, the site at which the tumour occurred was adjacent to the SMA; third, the fact that although all voluntary movements (including eye movements) were lost but automatic movements such as the ability to cough and swallow were maintained. The importance of coughing and swallowing is that it stops saliva from going down "the wrong way" into the lungs and causing an infection. In patients who have serious impairments in their consciousness this ability is often lost and can cause serious problems. The peculiar thing about Alex's SMAS is that it affected both sides, presumably because of the size and extent of the tumour, as well as the ability to voluntarily open her eyelids (*apraxia of lid opening*).

The importance of diagnosing SMAS is that there is usually a good prognosis. This means that patients can and do recover very well. While we suspected this all along, it was only in the fullness of time, when Alex started to improve dramatically, that it became clear it was SMAS all along. However strongly we rationalised that Alex's symptoms were going to get better, it was an anxious time for all involved.

Chapter 12

Reports from staff and Alex's former partner

Barbara A. Wilson

These interviews and reports are included to illustrate Alex's improvement over time. They are reported in chronological order.

Addenbrooke's hospital

Between 6 March and 10 April 2017, Alex was assessed by the neuropsychology department at Addenbrooke's hospital. The initial assessments were limited because of Alex's fatigue, severe perseveration and emotional lability. The assessments found Alex to have moderate to marked difficulties across all areas of executive functioning including impulsivity, inhibition, reduced verbal reasoning, poor planning and problem solving, initiation and motor sequencing difficulties. On an inhibition test she had a strategy in place but could not sustain it, making errors every few test items. While she performed in the mildly impaired range on an immediate verbal recall memory test, this was thought to be due to an attention deficit, as she frequently recalled the names in a confused/conflated way. Consistent with this, and on a more complex working memory task, she demonstrated difficulties holding onto and manipulating information in her mind. Qualitatively, she demonstrated good episodic memory for recent events and for having seen certain therapists. She performed well on tests of visuospatial functioning.

The neuropsychologists reported that over the past month, there had been an improvement in the frequency and severity of Alex's perseverative behaviours. She was also more able to initiate and engage in conversations. She continued to demonstrate some physical perseverations such as stroking her thighs continuously, picking up various items around her, and waving her arms up and down above her head. She benefited from regular pauses to break perseverative behaviour, including a total change of topic or activity; or from direct commands to break the physical movement, for example "put your hand in my hand". Her responses to questions were significantly faster. Whereas previously she required 20 to 30 seconds to respond, now she was responding instantly.

Over the past week or so there had been increased instances of sexually disinhibited behaviours, which can become a source of fixation. She displayed socially inappropriate behaviours such as breaking wind loudly, picking her nose, swearing and making explicit sexual comments, for example, asking a member of staff to engage in a threesome and commenting on a male nurse's boxer shorts. She can be overfriendly by, for example, hugging members of staff.

Qualitatively, her attentional abilities were inconsistent (as in keeping with frontal pathology). She had demonstrated that she was able to sit and engage in a group session for 30 minutes. At other times she presented as very distractible and impulsive, for example, getting up in the middle of a testing session, or discontinuing a session with no prior warning ("thank you, I have had enough now"). There were ongoing safety concerns surrounding her impulsivity during a recent home visit.

During the assessment there was some evidence of emotional lability. For example, she was observed to rub her leg and let out a pained cry, saying she felt like a toddler with bottled-up emotions. She reported being unable to control these emotions and that she had "empathy" with toddlers. She benefited from being asked to sit back in her chair, arms by her side and take a deep breath. She was aware that her mood and behaviour had changed and were now uncharacteristic of her premorbid personality. This had been quite upsetting for her and she had at times been quite tearful.

In June 2018 an interview was conducted with Hermione Thorp, speech and language therapist (SALT). Hermione used to work at Addenbrooke's and knew Alex when she was on the Lewin Unit. However, she felt she did not know Alex well and suggested we took more note of the report from the senior SALT (see her report below). Hermione was working with other patients but would see Alex on the ward. She remembered seeing her lying in bed, motionless, with her legs looking odd and thinking that she (Alex) didn't look comfortable. Then she remembered her not talking. She would be sitting in the dining room, not talking but with other people around. Hermione said Alex had definitely changed but she didn't remember details about the change. When she walked she looked unsteady on her feet. She would sometimes say inappropriate things but Hermione couldn't remember an example. The senior SALT said, one day, that she had taken Alex outside and Alex jumped on a fountain, making her worried that Alex would fall.

The following detailed report is from the senior speech and language therapist at Addenbrooke's hospital. The entire set of notes is reproduced as these illustrate Alex's recovery journey.

Senior SALT's notes

1–2 March 2017

During our first interactions on the Rehab ward, Alex was able to smile in response to the speech and language therapist (SALT) and give thumbs up when prompted, but she needed help to put her thumbs down between questions. Family reported that Alex had whispered sentences.

On our second meeting, the SALT trialled modelling a spoken "yes". Alex smiled and looked intently, opened her mouth, touched chin as if to help with speech, then touched her lower lip, rubbing it (it looked dry). During this session the SALT asked some questions, completing a background information form to help the team get to know Alex. A written yes/ no sheet was offered for Alex to point to, in order to answer closed questions. Alex pointed with her pen and circled the word, tending to get stuck on this action and repeating it. Alex was able to operate her iPad, but again tended to get stuck on actions such as selecting the date.

When open-ended questions were asked, given time, Alex wrote her answers, telling us she studied English Literature at the University of York, is now an eco-builder, building her own house in Cambridge with Mike.[1] She reported she met Mike at Schumacher College in Devon, where she studied for an MSc in Holistic Science, which led to an interest in eco-building and body movement. Alex was already practising yoga but had deepened her knowledge of this practice in India.

Language appeared relatively intact through writing, although further assessment was required. Alex had difficulty initiating responses at this stage; there was no vocalisation during this session, although Alex had seemed to make an attempt at purposeful oral movement in response to the SALT's "yes" model. Alex had difficulty shifting from one action to another, and benefited from gentle support to stop an action and move on to the next thing. Alex needed time in an interaction, and it helped to say her name before asking a question.

Our next session was over lunch in the dining room, with friends Katie and Mark. Alex fed herself mince, mash and peas, then apple crumble and custard. Alex tended to overload her fork, but responded when prompted to take less, with repetition. Prompts were also needed to help Alex stop one action, for example scraping the dish, and to move on to another spoonful or to put the cup down. The busy environment was probably distracting for Alex.

Earlier that day Alex had written that she was very keen to speak. She expressed much frustration during this meeting, gesturing with two fingers and writing "they all make the same mistake, treating me like a fool". The SALT offered reassurance that people did not think that, and apologised that it was making her feel this. Alex later wrote to the SALT and friend Katie, "don't infantilise me", following efforts to help her stop prolonged sucking from the hot chocolate cup. The SALT suggested writing communication guidelines together, to ensure that we could get communication right for Alex.

Following Mike's arrival, and discussion about a straw, Alex whispered "Replace it with something else" – these were the first spoken words heard by the SALT and fully appropriate to the conversation.

At this point the SALT suggested the following techniques to support Alex's communication:

- Ask one question at a time.
- Avoid multi-tasking or switching too quickly.
- Give time for Alex to reply.
- Alex may give thumbs up or down.
- Ensure pen and paper to hand for Alex to write.
- Help to move on if stuck on an action.
- Avoid talking too loudly or being patronising.

7 March 2017

Alex greeted the SALT on arrival, in short sentences with low volume (but not a whisper). She did not respond verbally to further social questions, but did write "yes" (that she had had breakfast). Alex then wrote about medications and drug trials. Clarification was needed, but it was possible that this was confabulation. The SALT redirected Alex to being here in hospital for rehabilitation.

With Alex's permission, the SALT supported her to put her iPod down, and to switch activity by moving pen and paper away – Alex was perseverating on writing a question mark.

We trialled a variety of methods to facilitate voluntary control over spoken output:

- Hum – brief and low in volume achieved × 3.
- Hum plus vowel "ee", not achieved.

- Phrase completion, for example "tea and coffee".
- Effortful – gave visual oral model. Alex completed (cof) "fee".

Alex was unable to complete phrases in direct response to the SALT's modelling and prompting, but after a delay she read out and completed all phrases accurately.

Trialled Speech Sounds on Cue APP: no spoken responses were elicited; it was possibly too quick/overloading with stimulation. Alex needed support to avoid pressing her iPad.

Counting, with tactile feedback using fingers – lots of repetition given but Alex did not join in with the SALT. It was possible that fatigue was impacting on Alex's ability to carry out the tasks.

The SALT fed back to Alex that she was producing more spoken language, and that a low voice was heard not just a whisper. Alex thanked the SALT for the feedback in writing and asked for a drink of water as she was thirsty (in writing).

Later that day, Alex's sister Debs, and Mike were visiting. We spoke about the morning's sessions and discussed the humming and music. Debs sang some familiar songs from childhood ("Right said Fred", "Dig a Hole", "Bear Necessities"). Alex was able to fill many gaps with a quiet voice or whisper.

9 March 2017

Alex was colouring in on the SALT's arrival and commented that she had drawn it herself and was practising doing it with her left hand. Alex agreed for SALT support to put it to one side. Alex was tapping with her hands; SALT held Alex's hand gently to support Alex and reduce this.

Alex greeted SALT with speech and was further able to respond to some direct questions today. During conversation, Alex was able to tell the SALT that she comes from Surrey, close to Guildford. Slow processing/delayed initiation was noted at times, but this was variable.

Rote speech tasks were carried out to help gain voluntary control of speech initiation: counting using fingers, 1–5 Alex held the SALT's fingers up. Alex counted in French, Spanish, German and Portuguese. In English, Alex was able to say the number when the SALT held up fingers, responding to the SALT's timing rather than counting in a whole 1–5 sequence. She was able to go backwards and to name which number finger the SALT held up in random order.

Alex returned to drawing after giving a written response in conversation. When the SALT asked whether she would like help to put it aside,

Alex wrote "No" and circled it. SALT noted to Alex that whilst we are trying to support Alex to stop activities she is stuck on, we may not always predict that accurately so she could let us know those times, as on this occasion.

16 March 2017

First session in SALT rooms rather than on the ward. Alex asked whether the SALT had learned the songs yet, so we looked up one on YouTube.

On sitting up to the computer, Alex began to log on with her own email address. Multiple typos were made, but self-corrected each time. SALT noted and repeated that it would need to be the SALT's log-on, but Alex continued to write her own details. Possibly unable to attend to the SALT's feedback during typing/or to stop the action. Later perseveration was noted on typing the speaker's words in the search bar of YouTube. SALT gave feedback, Alex continued the action, SALT offered directly to help her stop, Alex agreed it was helpful if we helped her to stop. The SALT took Alex's hands off the keyboard.

SALT navigated to the song, we sang together. Alex noted it did not interest her or motivate her. We discussed her preferences/potential communication goals:

- Alex would like to get back to where she was (in terms of communication).
- To talk about gardens, plants, Gaia theory.
- To be given subtle cues regarding communication (need to explore further).
- To talk with eye contact (computer may be distracting).

The SALT suggested Alex write a paragraph summary of key points of Gaia theory for the next session, to educate the SALT, who was unfamiliar with it. Alex noted she has realised she prefers learning to teaching.

During this session there was a significant increase in spoken output, with on-going perseveration during tasks and slow processing at times, but improvement noted in initiation and speed of many responses.

Further development of the communication goals was planned, including where to focus the "subtle cues" regarding communication.

(Alex, you have asked whether you were "pulling out clumps of hair" during this session – I recall that you would repetitively run your fingers through your hair, and that occasionally a strand would come

out as it would for anyone. I think it was one of the actions you would "get stuck" on. You may have been feeling the re-growth of your hair?)

22 March 2017

Noted on-going increasing initiation of communication and conversation.

Alex was kneeling on her bed on the SALT's arrival and agreed to go outside to Jubilee Gardens. Donned slippers and two jumpers with some prompting. Alex walked quickly, SALT held up in corridor by bed moving, SALT needed to call to Alex to wait.

Outside, Alex jumped on to the ledge of the sculpture, walking quickly round and round, commenting she had seen a little girl do the same. The SALT encouraged her to get down, giving her arm for support. Alex's left knee sunk low when she jumped and she commented that she needed to build her strength.

Voice: Alex commented on her monotone, asking whether it was improving. She reported that it had been mentioned to her. SALT gave feedback that it was still tending to be monotone, but that volume was much louder. We reflected that she was speaking more loudly above environmental noise.

Gaia theory: Alex stated she preferred to do the exercise verbally rather than in writing as previously suggested. Alex had some difficulty clearly summarising; support was given by requesting three key points.

Alex showed some impulsivity when outside with SALT, jumping on the sculpture and eating two small bites of forsythia flower and a different leaf. Alex complied when encouraged not to eat any more. Alex's interest in plants and holistic science was acknowledged, so this may not have been unusual for her, but was perhaps in this context. The team felt that Alex would benefit from being accompanied when she left the ward.

29 March 2017

Volume/tone

Increasing variation in tone and volume in Alex's conversational speech. Alex still tended to monotone speech but this was improving. As suggested by the family, we practised reading aloud with an "advertising voice", with prompts to think loud and go slowly. The SALT encouraged Alex to stand up and "present" to SALT, to encourage role play and voice projection. Alex started with good volume but became quieter over the course of the text, with speed increasing. We aimed to continue this exercise with poetry, to address variation in tone, pitch and volume.

Eye contact

Alex commented on giving eye contact, that she found it tiring. She noted that she may engage in other activities (looking at book, tapping), to enable her to look away. We discussed how it is usual to look away and then look back at the speaker. We noted that Alex gives a lot of eye contact (she felt she always has). Alex commented that she found multi-tasking difficult.

Behaviour

Alex noted she was behaving in a child-like way, more so around other patients and staff, less so with visitors. Alex noted that being in the patient role contributed to this and that she would like to behave in an adult way all the time. We planned to discuss further.

We discussed how the things Alex was experiencing can occur after brain injury, including finding it difficult to initiate and then to stop an activity, to multi-task, to switch attention, to "filter" comments (Alex's own word) and self-monitor.

Potentially useful strategies were identified

- Give Alex gentle prompts when she is stuck on a repetitive action, help her to stop.
- Help Alex to switch her focus of attention from one activity to the next with gentle prompts.

Alex identified the need for self-directed strategy for when she was going home, and to work towards this. Planned to discuss the "filter" further.

30 March 2017

Discussion about eating normal consistency foods (soft diet advised up to now), but avoiding distractions and avoiding foods which would be an obvious choking risk such as nuts.

13 April 2017

Read poetry that Alex had prepared, noted ongoing rapid speed but greater variety of intonation in reading and conversational speech.

Further discussion about communication interactions

Alex concerned she comes across as rude and doesn't intend this. Tearful. Misunderstandings occurring in conversation, with insufficient background information being given in conversations – Alex reported she knew this was due to her.

Some discussion raised by Alex about being very busy with therapy and visitors – too much at times, cancelling visitors but wanting to maintain friendships.

Communication advice refreshed to include:

- Reduce distractions.
- Help Alex to stop repetitive actions with gentle prompt or touch on hand.
- Ask Alex to explain further if misunderstandings occur.

19 April 2017

Met with Alex at bedside, chose to come to SALT rooms for session. Discussed:

- Improving variation in tone and pitch, although Alex feels worse when tired and still not usual for her.
- Alex has been thinking about openers and closers in conversation to help avoid coming across as rude – for example, "Excuse me".
- Alex noted she had sworn at Mike. Trying to filter this consciously, Alex labelled this as fake, "fake it till you make it".
- Alex reported feeling under pressure when they visited the local community garden; she chose to go off and look around.
- Alex felt she has lots of ideas about what to do; we discussed her running them by family and team members to get help with the "filter" or executive control, i.e. deciding whether it is a good idea.
- Eye contact – Alex noted she gives intense eye contact. Rehearsed looking away and then back again during conversation. To do this with others.

- Slowing down, mindful walking with Mike. Discussed how Alex tends to set off quickly, and she noted she sometimes turns her back on people whilst still talking. To work on walking together, being aware of others around her.
- Alex would like a timetable.
- Planned for eye contact prompts by all – remind re. aim of not giving too much eye contact, glance away and back again.
- Continue conversation and reflection re. filters.

26 April 2017

Therapy/family meeting – discussed goal areas:

- Physical fitness, ideally an outside activity.
- Cooking, preferably at home.
- To volunteer in a local community garden.
- Overnight leave – to discuss with OT.
- Singing with friend Anna.
- Dancing.
- Cognitive strategies to support achievement of goals.

28 April 2017

Met with Alex as arranged. Walked to SALT rooms together.

Alex reported on BIRT assessment that had taken place in the morning. Alex would like to visit BIRT herself to assess them.

When asked what she would like to discuss in the session, Alex reported that she actually needed to rest, she had some visitors coming later. We agreed to end the session, noting that it was good that she identified the need to rest in the moment and initiated it.

Planned to continue discussions re. eye contact, decision making, the social filter.

5 May 2017

Alex requested to go outside for the session; we sat in the Jubilee Gardens.

Discussion about Alex reporting to staff that other patients required reviews and updated advice sheets.

Alex raised this herself, noting that she had found if quite distressing as she had not slept well the previous night and had been worrying about the patients. She had noted a clear response from the doctors, that they would not discuss other patients with her, and had noted reticence when speaking to the therapists. She reported this had made her upset. We reflected that she had taken the cue from the therapists when the conversation was ended, with a reflection that we could see she was worrying about people. Reassurance was given at the time that all was in hand. Alex had spoken to her sister on the telephone and come to the conclusion that she would try not to do this; it was not her role, she should concentrate on her own recovery.

We spoke about roles and social and professional boundaries. Alex reported she is focusing on being empathetic with other patients in her bay.

We considered whether there was a strategy Alex could develop around this, for now noticing these things happening, and cues from others a good step.

Planned for ongoing communication style reflection

10 May 2017

Met with Alex on patio.

Alex reflected on how she had kept running in the gym despite another patient having become unwell, and that in retrospect she felt this may have been inappropriate. She noted she may have been in the way of people helping the patient. Alex noted she was enjoying the running, was being timed, had asked staff to give her maths questions whilst running.

We discussed a "Stop, think" strategy, acknowledging that Alex was probably able to work out what to do for the best, but had not been able to act on it in the moment, possibly due to difficulty switching tasks/stopping.

Alex noted she has many questions regarding radiotherapy – we discussed a strategy of writing down questions in preparation for the appointment and asking either the clinician or Mike to write down the answers for reflection.

Alex reported feeling she has more to achieve and therefore looking forward to BIRT, but does not like to dwell on problems, but rather positives. She understands there may be more feedback tomorrow re. BIRT and a stay of one month has been mentioned.

Plan: ongoing communication reflection/strategy work

Senior SALT, 16 November 2018

Dr Linda Crawford, clinical psychologist, met Alex when she was on the Lewin Unit at Addenbrooke's hospital. Linda also knew Alex at Fen House and described her memory of Alex as follows:

I saw Alex at the Lewin. She was very restless but practical and philosophical. There were multiple layers to her – she came across as chaotic; she jumped from one theme, one goal, to another. She wanted to please but she wasn't doing meaningful things. For her rehab was not about function. Initially she had problems with insight. She assumed she could do things. One of her goals was to "feel healing from the grass". That wasn't going to get her home! She was constantly negotiating. There were problems with her partner. Alex had been very unwell – she looked amazing but she was not as she was before. She never wanted to be back where she was before. She saw it, the illness, as part of her life's journey. She said "you can take me as I am – or don't take me".

This was a challenge for traditional rehab. It was more a question of explaining. It was a challenge for us and for them as a couple as well. She had been a high earner, making a lot of money on the one hand and her seeing herself as a hippy on the other hand.

Mike wanted her to be the high earner but also the hippy he had fallen in love with. Alex ripped the house apart as she wanted an eco-retrofit while Mike was thinking how is it going to look. David Ruthenberg, neuropsychologist, worked extensively with Alex. Mike needed lots of reassurance. David did a lot of the day-to-day work. There was anxiety about the discharge. What Mike wanted didn't really exist. The OZC came up, I'm not sure about the funding. I thought Alex wouldn't get funding. She was very dysexecutive at the time. She said that pre-injury she could communicate with butterflies.[2]

Fen House (Brain Injury Rehabilitation Trust: BIRT)

After Addenbrooke's, Alex went to the BIRT rehabilitation centre, Fen House. While there she saw Dr David Ruthenberg. His report appears below. Gemma Chaplin, a psychology assistant, also saw Alex at Fen House.

Report from David Ruthenberg

Alex arrived on the neuro-rehabilitation unit shortly before I did as a locum consultant clinical psychologist in neuropsychology. Our brief in the unit was to "get her as rehabbed as possible" prior to possible radiation therapy for post-surgery, residual tumour cells. My specific brief was to engage therapeutically with Alex as she was deemed not to require extensive neuropsychological assessment based on overall functionality as per staff observations, but more particularly given the neuro-radiological brief. However, over time and as part of my observations, there were concerns with regard to aspects of executive functions, notably aspects of interpersonal and general judgement and a subtle degree of disinhibition and possible mood regulatory problems, which became apparent over time. However, my involvement was to include close observation clinically of these and other issues which may have required formal quantitative psychological assessment. However, the overarching brief was therapeutic and to facilitate Alex being able to make an informed decision about possible further medical treatment.

I began seeing Alex on a weekly basis for hour-long sessions. She managed these sessions with ease and indeed prepared, usually in writing, discussion subjects of relevance. Initially, I wished merely to engage with her and to enable her to feel contained and safe and to lay the foundations for an assessment of her baseline levels of qualitative judgement, her emotional regulation, insight and judgement and interpersonal functioning and to monitor her overall neuropsychological functioning.

However, even on our first meeting, sitting on the lawn in the sun, it was clear that she was both looking for and able to appreciate subtle understanding and interpretation of aspects of her presentation. For instance, even at that first meeting, I was able to suggest to her that she seemed to be pushing herself to function rather like the high-functioning professional she had been prior to her surgery when her actual capacities at the time clearly lagged behind such functional desires. She was aware of my psycho-analytic background (she had been informed of this when she first arrived) and I wondered whether she was keen to meet me at that level as it were, notwithstanding her actual needs and levels of functioning.

Despite being told that the odds of the recurrence of any cancer after radiation treatment were negligible, especially relative to her not having such treatment, Alex was extremely ambivalent about having it. There was considerable pressure on her, especially from her highly supportive family, to have the treatment and this proved to be the defining issue throughout her stay. My role in this regard was extremely difficult. She looked to me for support on the one hand and, at worst, to remain neutral on the subject. However, given the extreme odds favouring treatment over not, such a position would effectively have been unprofessional. At the same time, there was no evidence that her position was owing to her neuropsychological status. Alex and her partner had quite clear, untraditional ideas about many things including allopathic medicine. From the outset of our contact, there was an implicit assumption that I, too, would support an unconventional approach. Alex had quite legitimate concerns about the radiation treatment affecting other central structures. However, to my judgement, such concerns, while objectively valid, really were rationalisations for her "essential" position of not wishing to have the treatment as a matter of principle.

However, this issue served to focus more of my time with her and the various couple and family meetings which I facilitated. In these meetings, my role changed somewhat; to be supportive of Alex on the one hand but to guide the discussion so that Alex's voice could be clearly heard. It was my view that she would see the sense in having the treatment *if* she felt that her opposition (and anxieties) to it was clearly heard. At the personality level, Alex revealed a stubborn and to an extent a rather rigid set of personality characteristics. I felt that she could become obstructively oppositional if she felt others were trying to tell her what to do and would refuse to undergo the treatment for these reasons.

There were also reports of arguments or disagreements with her partner when at home for weekend leave. Again, there was uncertainty as to whether she was demonstrating emotional dysregulation or whether the demands being made of her at home were owing to her surface functionality being mistaken for her "being back to her old self", which she was not. The line to tread was narrow and precarious.

Alex had arrived at the unit with a history of having been a high-flying fundraiser for a variety of off-centre projects, but successfully securing money from highly traditional sources. Her strength of character, doggedness, articulateness and intelligence served both as a reassurance, but also, at times, difficult to penetrate when her thinking, rigidity and strongly held position regarding some form of alternative treatment in Barcelona for instance, may have been influenced by her neurological status.

As matters developed and the closer decision time came, the greater the pressure on her grew and the more important my role as trusted and informed support for her became. A lasting memory of her was of the final family session, where member after family member encouraged her to have the treatment. She had divulged to me her interest in the alternative treatment in Spain and, as I recall, I was to speak to the clinician involved. But within myself, I was clear that she should have the treatment offered her at Addenbrooke's. My sense of betraying her was near agonizing as I had to declare my position, leaving Alex to be a lone fighter for her values and principles.

I left the service before knowing the outcome, but as I understand it she went through with the treatment and is making a steady recovery. She will remain as someone whom I both deeply respect and whose courage to stand by her principles in the face of life-and-death odds was salutary.

Further reports

In August 2017, Alex went to see Dr Kirker, the consultant in rehabilitation in charge of the Lewin Unit at Addenbrooke's. He reported that she felt safe alone at home, was able go out independently to shops and follow a naturopathic diet. Alex's partner reported that multi-tasking remains difficult and Alex must not be interrupted during a task, for example while making a cup of tea. She needed peace and silence, and conversation and written material had to be very focused. She was cycling to the shops wearing a helmet. She continued with yoga and was about to go on a retreat for 31 days to Somerset to a cancer recovery centre with a naturopathic diet. She had a seizure when she omitted pills in June but was currently seizure free. She was having daily radiotherapy with one week remaining. She had a new wig. Although tired, her mood was good. Her partner felt Alex was emotionally brittle and cried when she met certain people or if she was contradicted or had a request declined. In October Dr Kirker asked the neuro OT if she thought a referral to the OZC was appropriate.

An interview with Gemma Chaplin, who knew Alex both from Fen House and from the OZC, was conducted in May 2018. Gemma said:

> I worked with Alex in the kitchen. She was very thorough and wanted to create healthy salads. One of the main differences here (at the OZC) is that she doesn't talk as much now, she is more aware of turn taking. At BIRT you couldn't get a word in edgeways. She was very disinhibited there. I remember one of the physiotherapists saying that Alex wanted to lead the sessions and engage in childlike play. This may be part of her personality but she was too disinhibited like wanting to do cartwheels. I remember she struggled when people offered help. She didn't want help, she wanted to get on with things by herself; she was very independent. Mike tried to help but Alex wanted to do things her own way. She was very playful but also more tearful at BIRT. Of course, at that time she had just come out of hospital. She always seemed confident, then and now.

The final interview was with Mike, Alex's partner. He was seen in August 2018. He was asked when he first noticed something was wrong. He said,

> Alex was feeling depressed. Her personality had always been bubbly – it was one of the things I most admired about her. She was borderline cheeky, lots of social capacity. I think she started to have a few headaches in the last quarter of 2015. She went to acupuncture – she's

always been a self-starter. The year before we ate the same sea food, she became ill; we thought she had an infection because I wasn't ill. The same thing happened in 2016, we just thought it was an upset tummy. This is where, with hindsight, things became evident. She had a mild depression, she just wasn't as sociable as before. She wanted to retreat, be at home instead of being the outgoing person she was. Then there were the headaches. She wanted to be alone. Something was off kilter, I'm not sure what. In mid-January 2017, she had been vomiting for a few days, then she had a strong bout of vomiting. It looked horrible. I sat her on the bed and she had a dazed look as if to say "Where am I?" She could not speak. I could see she could understand, but she couldn't answer although she could nod. There was a childlike demeanour to her eyes. That's when I called the G.P and he said to take her to hospital. I took her to Addenbrooke's. She vomited on the way there. She was seen quickly at A&E. She was still vomiting. They did a CT scan of her brain and then said "You had better take a seat". The doctor on duty said, "There's a mass in your brain; you are going to spend the night here." We learned she had a tumour, a meningioma. They kept her in for two nights. The first night there, Adel Helmy said it was a normal tumour, the kind we are used to dealing with but this was abnormally large. It is a slow-growing tumour and may have been there for several years! We will have to operate; it is urgent but not an emergency. Come back in two weeks. Alex said, "Thank god I am not depressed. I have a tumour." The next two weeks we were in an awkward kind of limbo. We were told a range of healing times. We thought she would be out a week after the operation. They gave her steroids to stop the vomiting.

On 14 February 2017 Alex was admitted to Addenbrooke's. She was in a good mood and filled with hope. We knew it was dangerous but thought she was in capable hands. I went home and waited for them to call in the evening, which they did. It wasn't a benign tumour as we expected. Alex came round, she could communicate with her eyes; she had an incredibly painful face. She had no control of her body. Five days afterwards, Alex began to have a little movement. There was no speech at first. Nine days later she was able to write something. She went to the Lewin Unit on 28 February and on 7 March, there was the first whisper. She started to have hallucinations or delusions. I worked in the mornings and then in the afternoons and evenings I went to the Lewin. After a few days, they let me help so I looked after her. She developed conspiratorial theories.

Two weeks after the operation, after physiotherapy, Adel Helmy came in and said it was a malignant growth, a grade three tumour, and there would always be cells so she had to move to the Oncology department. This was a severe blow to our morale. This battle had just started. Alex was completely helpless. It took a lot of energy and effort; she was like a child, but in no time she recovered. It was beautiful to watch. Every day she regained something. On 10 March I took her to the concourse (in Addenbrooke's) in a wheelchair. On 17 March she was walking with assistance but still speaking very little. On 26 March she was allowed out of hospital for a drive.

She needed radiotherapy but the oncologist said she was too weak for that and she had to wait until she was strong enough. It was after BIRT that the radiotherapy started – so months later. She persevered with her speech and on 2 April she was talking relatively well. She was allowed to have weekends away from 23 April. She returned Sunday night. She left the Lewin on 11 May and went to BIRT on 15 May. She stayed for six weeks, then home to Cambridge and then six weeks of radiotherapy,

Alex had her first seizure at BIRT. It was very traumatic for me and very ugly. It is hard to see the person you love, so frail. She had a second seizure too. They lasted 10–20 seconds. The first time I did resuscitation. Calling an ambulance on the A14 is not nice. It was a watershed – seeing her so helpless and vulnerable. She had the radiotherapy five times a week, Monday to Friday. There was a huge debate within the family. Alex wasn't certain she wanted it and it took a lot of persuasion from the whole family. The neuro-oncologist said there would be minimal brain damage, but he couldn't say how much. I think the hippocampus was the most affected. We weren't expecting a personality change – that surprised us. We were told there were mild cognitive difficulties. We were surprised that the medical profession was most concerned with the risk of the disease coming back, and not with quality of life. There were all sorts of repercussions. We decided to split up because of the personality change. She recovered well from the surgery but the radiotherapy was a kick too far. There has been a fundamental change in her.

We have had excellent support from the OZC and from BIRT.

Alex has done extremely well. She is currently very independent, looks absolutely normal and is outgoing and sociable. Probably much as she was before she became ill.

Notes

1 Alex notes, "I was not building a house, I was doing an eco-retrofit, putting in insulation and replacing cement with new lime plaster, for example."

2 Note from Alex: I didn't actually say this but did think I could communicate with birds in the early days – I still believe this happened. And I know from personal experience that humans and plants can communicate, though not necessarily in language.

Chapter 13

Alex at the Oliver Zangwill Centre

Barbara A. Wilson

Why did Alex come to the OZC?

Alex sustained damage to both frontal lobes during the surgery. The frontal lobes are responsible for planning, organisation, problem solving, selective attention, personality, behaviour and emotions. The anterior part of the frontal lobe, the prefrontal cortex, has an important role in higher cognitive functions and personality. The posterior area of the frontal lobe consists of pre-motor and motor areas. It controls the movement on the opposite side of the body, predominantly via the pre-central gyrus (Wilson, Dhamapurker & Rose, 2016). The lower region of the frontal lobe immediately in front of the pre-central gyrus controls the expression of speech. Damage to both frontal lobes may produce an alteration in personality, a loss of normal inhibitions and incontinence. Alex had many of these problems as can be seen from the various reports in Chapter 12. Indeed, she was diagnosed with Supplementary Motor Area (SMA) Syndrome, a syndrome associated with damage to the frontal lobes.

What is SMA Syndrome? Although this syndrome has been described by Adel Helmy in Chapter 11, a few extra words are probably advisable here. SMA Syndrome occurs following damage to the supplementary motor area; such damage frequently appears after surgery to remove tumours (Bannur & Rajshekhar, 2000). Characteristics of the syndrome include reduction of spontaneous movements and difficulty in performing voluntary motor acts to command. This happens despite muscle tone in the limbs being maintained or increased (ibid.). Speech deficits may or may not be seen. Bannur and Rajshekhar (2000) describe six patients who underwent surgery for removal of a tumour in the SMA and say that as well as "a severe impairment of volitional movements, the salient features of the deficits in this syndrome are hemineglect and dyspraxia or apraxia involving the contralateral limbs" (p. 204). All of the patients in this study went on to *regain* their lost functions, as did six of eight patients reported by Ibe et al. (2016). Alex, too, regained speech and voluntary control of her limbs. The return of these functions can be seen in the reports of those who worked with her as described in the previous chapter. Another common consequence of frontal lobe damage, however, is difficulty with executive functioning.

What are executive deficits?

In the words of Goldberg (2001: 23), "A patient with frontal lobe disease will retain the ability to move around, use language, recognise objects, and even memorize information. Yet like a leaderless army, cognition disintegrates and ultimately collapses with the loss of the frontal lobes." Executive functions are to do with planning, organisation, regulation and verification of activity, goal formulation and carrying out goal-directed plans effectively (Luria, 1966; Lezak, 1983). At one time people with such problems were said to have Frontal Lobe Syndrome but Baddeley (1986) thought it odd to call a syndrome after an anatomical region so coined the term "dysexecutive syndrome" (DES) to describe the nature of the impairment arising from frontal lobe damage. Baddeley and Wilson (1988), based on Rylander (1939), said the main characteristics of DES were 1) impairments in attention (people were easily distracted), 2) difficulty grasping the whole of a complicated state of affairs, and 3) people with DES may be able to work along routine lines, but would have difficulties in new situations. Assessments and observations showed that Alex was left with just such difficulties: that is to say she had marked executive deficits and because of these required rehabilitation. As we have seen, her rehabilitation began at the Lewin Unit in Cambridge, then continued at Fen House in Ely before ending at the OZC. Dr Kirker began making enquiries about treatment at the OZC in August 2017; he, together with Dr Aneesh Shravat of the local cancer care centre, made the referral to the OZC originally for cognitive assessment and advice. Alex attended for this assessment in October and December 2017 (fuller description below) and began the full programme in January 2018. These are now reported in more detail.

First assessment at the OZC

Dr Jessica Fish, clinical psychologist, and Mrs Susan Brentnall, OT, saw Alex for a two-and-a-half-hour assessment in October 2017. On the basis of the findings and following discussions with Dr Shravat, it was decided to carry out further assessments with a view to determining if Alex was suitable for the full OZC programme. An additional half-day clinical interview, functional assessment and family interview was carried out in December 2017.

Much of the social history is covered elsewhere, but it is interesting to note that Dr Fish said that Alex had some memories of being unable to communicate while in hospital as part of the SMA Syndrome. She said she had been under the illusion that she was talking and that she was performing research. She said it was a month before she was able to resume walking. She received residential neurorehabilitation at BIRT for six weeks during May and June, and after this underwent a six-week course of radiotherapy with three-monthly reviews. She went on a one-month retreat to a centre in Somerset in the autumn of 2017 and eats a naturopathic diet.

Alex experienced some seizures during the immediate recovery period and a further one in June while on leave from BIRT. This seizure was witnessed and was a tonic-clonic seizure described by Dr Kirker as a medication withdrawal seizure possibly linked to a high emotion event. Alex wanted to reduce her current anti-convulsive medication and planned to discuss this once she had been seizure free for 12 months. (Note: at the time of writing in early 2019, this still has not happened although Alex is now on a very low dose of anti-convulsant medicine). At the time of her neuropsychological assessment, Alex was attending a cancer care service. This included drop-in sessions and some yoga sessions.

When attending for the assessment, Alex was neither working nor driving. She was, however, independent in use of public transport, in personal care and in in the domestic activities of daily living. She said that complex and/or novel tasks such as dealing with correspondence were more difficult for her, and she may procrastinate over these. She had resumed some of her former hobbies and activities.

Thus physically she had made a good recovery, although she suffered from physical and mental fatigue. Cognitively, Alex said she had concentration and memory difficulties. She was still impulsive, although she felt this had improved over the past few months. Nevertheless, she could still come across as rude when she did not mean to be. Her records noted that she displayed "utilisation behaviour" or environmental dependency syndrome (this is where someone reacts inappropriately to objects in the environment such as picking up someone else's comb and using it to comb their hair). Alex said that this had much improved but she still noticed the "edges" of this problem. For example, if she felt compelled to complete an action prompted by an object or situation, she could talk herself through it rather than act on the urge.

Alex was not depressed but did experience some anxiety, which was not surprising given her situation. She described some occasional obsessive-compulsive behaviours plus some decreased emotional control such as irritation, shouting and tearfulness. Her partner described her as being "more up and down than before, and more down than up". She also showed more distress, more difficulty socialising, reduced confidence and less assertion than usual.

Alex's behaviour was appropriate during the assessment and she seemed motivated to do well, although she became tearful when describing some of her problems.

The conclusions to the cognitive assessment suggested that Alex was of superior intellectual ability premorbidly. Her verbal skills were still very good, but she had problems with non-verbal reasoning and divided attention skills. These were in the borderline range of ability. Her speed of information processing was in the low average range. Her performance on tests of memory was variable with impaired recall and poor recognition. This was characteristic of the lesion sustained in the surgery. There was some evidence of reduced verbal generation and inhibitory control relative to the premorbid estimate, which was considered consistent with the reported problems with executive function, even though her scores on the structured tests were within the normal range.

As part of the functional assessment, Alex was observed completing a computer-based task involving accessing information from the internet to arrange a hypothetical social event, an evening out in London. The purpose of the task was to assess her cognitive abilities such as attention, planning and organisation on a task likely to be similar to that encountered in everyday life. Alex was given written instructions outlining the task parameters. She said this was a familiar task for her and that she knew London well as she used to live there. She was observed to be quick using the computer, her typing was also rapid and she only made the occasional spelling mistake which she corrected promptly. She used appropriate words and phrases in the search engine. She was able to complete the task independently, asking appropriate questions to clarify information. It was fed back to her that on one occasion she did not gain all the necessary information and had to go back to the original source (i.e. although she looked for performance times, she neglected to check for travel times). However, she was able to resolve this quickly as she left all the used tabs open. The therapist spoke and asked questions throughout the task, which Alex was able to deal with. She only once asked the therapist to be quiet so she could complete one element of the task. Alex slightly underestimated how long the task would take. As far as her fatigue was concerned she rated this as 7/10 at the beginning and 6/10 at the end, commenting that the task helped her fatigue.

Alex was asked what she found most challenging in terms of everyday functioning and she replied that she could "over complete things", that is to say, she followed through all the steps in a sequence even when all steps were not required. She also said she had communication difficulties being aware she was not as quick in conversation now and she could cut people off as she sometimes jumped in to make sure she did not forget something. She sometimes misunderstood what was being said and would like to be more articulate and improve her voice. She was aware she found things more challenging if many things were happening at once like trying to cook a meal. Another problem was that she put things off such as dealing with correspondence. She particularly wanted to learn about why she was experiencing the difficulties she had as this would stimulate her and improve her recovery. In summary, she completed most of the elements on the computer task including arranging the travel, the venue and the accommodation for an evening out. She kept within the budget, was able to write out her plan as requested and rate her fatigue levels (although she needed to be reminded to do this at the end of the session). It was felt that she should be assessed on a completely novel task.

The assessment concluded that the clear cognitive, emotional and physical consequences of Alex's brain injury had been identified. Cognitively, she had reduced non-verbal reasoning, speed of information processing, divided attention and memory. In the domain of emotions and behaviour, she had reduced ability to regulate her emotions and exhibited disinhibition. Physically, she experienced significant fatigue impacting on daily function. These changes interact with each other (for example, fatigue exacerbating difficulties with emotional regulation), and present an adjustment challenge. This challenge was causing distress and a threat to Alex's sense of identity, which in turn reduced her self-confidence. These interacting cognitive, emotional and physical consequences of brain injury were thought to warrant an interdisciplinary approach and, as such, it was recommended that Alex participate in the holistic programme of the OZC.

In a telephone feedback session with Alex and her partner it was agreed that the primary focus would be the six-week intensive programme, combining group and individual psycho-education and therapy sessions to facilitate Alex's understanding of her injury and its consequences in a therapeutic milieu and to identify rehabilitation goals and strategies to progress towards achieving these. The nature and intensity of subsequent rehabilitation input would be determined according to need and by the treating team in collaboration with Alex towards the end of the intensive phase.

Alex accepted her place on the programme and expressed enthusiasm for learning about herself in relation to her injury and for being with other people who have been through similar experiences. The next programme was due to start on 8 January 2018.

The programme

During the first six weeks, Alex was expected to attend from 10 a.m. to 4 p.m., Monday to Thursday. Her individual personal co-ordinator (IPC) was Dr Pieter du Toit, a clinical psychologist. This was a psycho-educational programme focusing on a different topic each week. Week 1 was an introduction to rehabilitation; week 2 was about understanding brain injury; week 3 addressed attention and memory; week 4 tackled executive functioning; week 5 was about communication and week 6 concerned mood. The groups were held in the mornings with individual sessions in the afternoon.

During induction week, Alex settled into the routine at the centre, became acquainted with the other people in her group and learned how the centre runs. It was also an opportunity to make sure all the practical arrangements like accommodation and taxis were running smoothly, should she require them. She was given a timetable for each week. She was reminded that she was likely to experience some apprehension about starting this programme and that it was natural to feel this way. She was reassured that the staff would do everything possible to help her feel relaxed and comfortable.

After completing the initial six-week period of rehabilitation, Alex was told she would begin the next phase, the integration phase, and this would happen following discussion with Dr du Toit. There would be a strong focus on implementing the strategies learned during the six-week introductory period at the OZC, in her home community.

Alex was informed that there would be meetings between herself, her family and the team to set goals and review progress, both at the end of the first six weeks and at the end of her rehabilitation programme. After completing the programme there would be review meetings with Alex and her family after three, six and 12 months

Support for relatives

The OZC team's acknowledgement that families play an important role in rehabilitation made it important for everyone to work together closely. Alex was told that the staff tried to achieve this in the following ways:

- Alex would be given a regular chance to talk with her IPC via weekly or fortnightly telephone calls.
- Free educational days for relatives and for children whose parents had sustained a brain injury would be provided on the subject of "Understanding Brain Injury".
- Family therapy sessions could be arranged with Alex and her family members or for family members alone as required.
- Family days would take place at least twice during the programme. The first one would be in induction week on Thursday 11 January. This would be a full day from 10 a.m. to 4 p.m. with lunch included and Alex was asked to let the team know if she was able to be involved in this and who would be attending from her family.
- The final family day would be decided nearer the time. This would also be a full day (10 a.m. to 4 p.m.) and include a UBI ("Understanding Brain Injury") workshop in the morning, support group for families and a review session in the afternoon. For those travelling longer distances, we hoped to schedule a progress meeting on this date if appropriate. Lunch would be provided.

Following assessment, discussion and interviews, a formulation was made of Alex's situation. This can be seen in Figure 13.1.

Alex's goals were negotiated between her, Dr du Toit and other members of the team. The goals set were 1) to learn about myself and my injury, 2) to be with other people with similar experiences, 3) to improve my voice and articulate myself better, and 4) to increase my confidence. By the end of the programme, Alex had achieved these goals. In addition to the goals a number of core outcome domains were identified. These included

> enrich my relationship with my partner; maximise health and fitness: return to meaningful activity; develop a greater understanding of the impact of my injury on my cognitive functioning; improve my cognitive functioning with respect to planning and complex problem solving, prospective memory etc.; be less self-critical and judgemental and more accepting; improve my emotional regulation skills regarding anxiety and irritability.

Alex rated her success on these domains herself and, although they improved, she continued to work on them. To illustrate some of the ways these domains were achieved see Table 13.1.

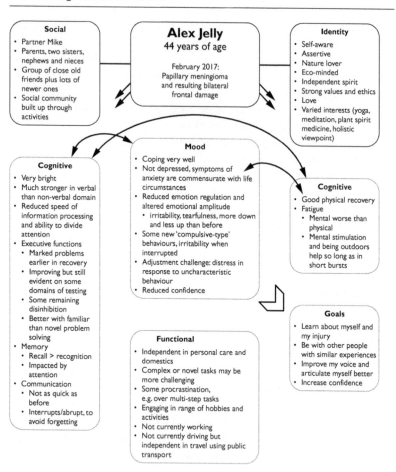

Figure 13.1 Alex's collaborative formulation.

It was evident to the staff working with her that Alex had grown in confidence. Furthermore, her ability to juggle multiple and competing demands in everyday life had improved through the application of various cognitive and practical strategies that she had learned. She also made very good use of alternative therapies and her access to the herbalism course she arranged herself and engaged in during her rehabilitation contributed to the overall process of self-discovery. Alex stressed that she felt over-tested and that the "story" aspects were more important to her. We should recognise the value of narrative and sense-making work as part of rehabilitation. The writing of this book has also been of therapeutic relevance for

Table 13.1 Some of the ways Alex's domains were achieved

Domains	Illustrative outcomes/interventions
1. Enrich my relationship with my partner	For example, Alex and her partner attended couples' sessions and decided to separate in the course of Alex's rehabilitation.
2. Maximise health and fitness	For example, Alex pursued a healthy diet and activities (e.g. yoga etc.) alongside her rehabilitation programme.
3. Return to meaningful activity	For example, Alex explored a variety of roles and activities that she found meaningful. She explored resuming her involvement at organisations such as 10 : 10 and commenced an intensive herbalism course. Additionally, she commenced co-authoring a book with Professor Barbara Wilson on her experiences during her illness and rehabilitation, as well as other creative writing projects.
4. Develop a greater understanding of the impact of my injury on my# cognitive functioning (Understanding Brain Injury – UBI)	For example, she met with a visiting scholar neurosurgeon, who provided her with information on her brain scan and treatment. She attended UBI sessions and drew on what she had learned in the abovementioned writing projects.
5. Improve cognitive functioning with respect to planning and complex problem solving, prospective memory etc.	For example, Alex developed various cognitive strategies suited to her particular requirements (as discussed further below).
6. Be less self-critical and judgmental and more accepting	For example, Alex reported positively on individual psychological therapy sessions.
7. Improve my emotion regulation skills (re. anxiety, irritability)	For example, Alex reported a greater capacity for emotion regulation and equanimity in the course of her rehabilitation.

Alex as it has consolidated the progress she has made in understanding and overcoming the difficulties caused by her tumour as well as enabling her to feel more secure and confident within her post-injury identity.

At the time of writing (early 2019), Alex reported that she has not yet been seizure free for 12 months, but is only on one Keppra a day (250 mg), which her consultant says is a non-therapeutic dose.

Chapter 14

Summary and conclusions

Barbara A. Wilson

This book is based upon the experience of a patient suffering from a growth in her brain, its subsequent removal by surgery, and the continuing account of the long days, weeks and months heading towards recovery. A considerable part of this book's pertinence lies in the fact that the words in Part I are written by the patient, Alex Jelly, herself. We are given a vivid account of her experiences, perceptions, memories, and interactions between herself and other patients, hospital staff, and her friends and relations as she progresses from an anxious individual worried by strange symptoms, to medical diagnosis, actual surgery and long days of rehabilitation. It helps that the author is a talented writer, an ex-student of literature and keen observer of life's mysteries, as well as being a student of varied philosophies and alternative ways of living. Her previous experiences give her writing an edge of insight that is rarely seen in other patient accounts. There is much humour, too, as Alex has a talent for finding and mocking the comedy she finds in errors, many of which can be found in all hospitals.

Initially, we are given an account of Alex's life as a talented student searching for better ways of living and trying out various ways of achieving fulfilment in work, much of it connected with charitable organisations. After experiencing feelings of fatigue and depression, Alex eventually goes for an examination at Addenbrooke's hospital in Cambridge where she learns she has a growth in her brain: a tumour, thought at first to be benign but later discovered to be a rare, malignant tumour known as a papillary meningioma, which she describes later as "the Lime in the Coconut". The operation is discussed by Alex and a further chapter describes the immediate after-effects.

The heart of the book is indeed Alex's prolonged description of her recovery from the operation and all the concomitant physical and psychological difficulties she has to overcome. It is an extraordinary story which contains accounts of her life before her operation, her early symptoms, diagnosis, the operation itself, how it felt to be paralysed for a while, and life on the ward at Addenbrooke's hospital and several other rehabilitation units. There are extremely funny observations of the various encounters between patients and staff and between patients themselves. The account is a mixture of reality, analysis, surreal interpretations, philosophy – and even creative writing, including a number of short stories and ideas for further development. She writes about her visitors, including character descriptions and a few verbal assassinations! Her stories are described as being about "life as seen through her psychosis". Alex also describes how she learned to walk again and praises the physiotherapists for their expertise and direct help.

"What can you teach me?" became her constant question to her friends and anyone who came her way. "I thought I could come out of this stronger and better than when I went in, and could pick up skills from anyone and everyone." Alex also writes quite extensively about the paranoia she experienced during her psychotic periods, which created difficulties for everybody on the ward. Alex picked on one nurse and claimed she was spying on her. When the nurse explained she was just enjoying the sunshine whilst eating her lunch, Alex thought, "Aha! That's exactly what a spy would say!"

Alex continued her later rehabilitation at a number of institutions including the Lewin Unit, the Brain Injury Rehabilitation Unit, Maggie's Wallace, Amchara, and the Oliver Zangwill Centre. Each are described, and their philosophies, methodologies and institutional differences are commented upon. One thing remains constant throughout and that is that Alex continued to have conversations with herself about her daily progress, recorded here in great detail thus providing the reader with an astonishingly in-depth account of her advance towards recovery. The nurses and therapists noticed her will to get better and their comments were picked up by Alex and turned over and over as she wondered whether they thought she had egotistic assumptions about being special, believing she was saved! Alex describes her love of movement and how much she enjoyed the dance classes, especially as movement was so much part of her life previously. She also participated in yoga with much enthusiasm and rigorously absorbed knowledge from information sessions organised by staff, which included cognitive behavioural therapy, Environmental Dependence Syndrome, perseveration and confabulation.

Alex learned about Environmental Dependence Syndrome, and how to stop responding inappropriately to stimuli in the environment. She also came to understand what perseveration and confabulation meant. She attended a monthly brain injury support group at Maggie's Wallace and enjoyed there the peaceful solitude she had not found in previous, more intense rehabilitation. At the Oliver Zangwill Centre, which Alex describes as the best rehabilitation unit she attended, she underwent a programme alongside other people who had suffered brain injury and appreciated that "being altogether" instilled high levels of confidence. Each week, for the first six weeks, the programme covered one topic. These were (1) an induction, which included other members of the family, (2) understanding brain injury, (3) attention and memory, (4) communication, (5) executive function and (6) mood. The best part of each week was when Alex would learn something that told her she was "normal" – that damage to the frontal lobes, for example, leads to loss of the abstract attitude when you come at things from the wrong perspective and failed to adapt. This was "music to Alex's ears". For the remainder of the programme, Alex attended two days a week while integrating into her normal everyday life.

The final chapters in Part I describe the various "alternative" therapies Alex tried out such as naturopathy, herbalism, acupuncture, network spinal analysis, yoga nidra and hyperbaric oxygen therapy. She also writes about her family and the many friends who offer her love and advice, including Mike, no longer the companion who gave her so much support through the darkest of days in rehabilitation but who remains a good friend. Alex, now fully active physically and mentally as witnessed by this remarkable book she has written, ends her story by writing: "I'm living proof that one can go through SMA Syndrome, psychosis, and rare, aggressive brain cancer and not only succeed but also have a normal life again."

Alex's story in Part I is followed in Part II with background information from Adel Helmy, Alex's neurosurgeon at Addenbrooke's hospital, and Barbara A. Wilson, clinical neuropsychologist and founder of the Oliver Zangwill Centre. Mr Helmy discusses meningiomas and Supplementary Motor Area Syndrome while Professor Wilson discusses reports and interviews with professional staff involved in the case as well as Alex's time at the OZC.

Finally, we hope readers will enjoy what we regard as one of the fullest, most perceptive and sharp-witted accounts ever of recovery from the mental, physical and social damage caused by a brain tumour as conveyed by Alex herself.

References

Baddeley, A. D. (1986) *Working Memory*. Oxford: Oxford University Press.

Baddeley, A. D. & Wilson, B. A. (1988) Frontal amnesia and the dysexecutive syndrome. *Brain and Cognition*, 7, 212–230.

Bannur, U. & Rajshekhar, V. (2000) Post operative supplementary motor area syndrome: clinical features and outcome, *British Journal of Neurosurgery*, 14(3), 204–210.

Cancer Research UK (n.d.) Side effects of radiotherapy. Retrieved from www.cancerresearchuk.org/about-cancer/brain-tumours/treatment/radiotherapy/long-term-side-effects

Classical Yoga (n.d.) Yoga Nidra. Retrieved from https://classicalyoga.co.uk/about-yoga-nidra

Coles, C., Williams, M. & Burnet, N. (1999) Hyperbaric oxygen therapy: Combination with radiotherapy in cancer is of proved benefit but rarely used. *British Medical Journal*, 318(7190), 1076–1077.

Doidge, N. (2016). *The Brain's Way of Healing: Stories of Remarkable Recoveries and Discoveries*. New York: Penguin Random House.

Double-slit experiment. (n.d.) Wikipedia. Retrieved from https://en.wikipedia.org/wiki/Double-slit_experiment

Escher, M. C. (1971) *The Graphic Work of M. C. Escher*. Ballantine.

Gawande, A. (2002) *Complications: A Surgeon's Notes on an Imperfect Science*. London: Profile Books.

Gladwell, M. (2008) *Outliers: The Story of Success*. Boston: Little, Brown and Company,

Goldberg, E. (2001) *The Executive Brain: Frontal Lobes and the Civilized Mind*. New York: Oxford University Press.

Harvey, M. (2005) *The Hole in the Sum of My Parts*. Suffolk: Poetry Trust.

Hughes, N. & Owen, F. (2018) *Weeds in the Heart*. Aeon Books and Quintessence Press

Ibe, Y., Tosaka, M., Horiguchi, K., Sugawara, K., Miyagishima, T., Hirato, M. & Yoshimoto, Y. (2016) Resection extent of the supplementary motor area and post-operative neurological deficits in glioma surgery. *British Journal of Neurosurgery*, 30(3), 323–329.

Keswick Jencks, M. (1995) *A View from The Front Line*. Retrieved from www. maggiescentres.org/media/uploads/publications/other-publications/view-from-the-front-line.pdf

Lambert, T. (n.d.) *A Brief History of Toilets*. Retrieved from www.localhistories. org/toilets.html

Levine, B., Robertson, I. H., Clare, L., Carter, G., Hong, J., Wilson, B. A., Duncan, J. & Stuss, D. T. (2000) Rehabilitation of executive functioning: An experimental-clinical validation of Goal Management Training. *Journal of the International Neuropsychological Society*, 6, 299–312.

Lezak, M. (1983) *Neuropsychological Assessment*, second edn. Oxford: Oxford University Press.

Luria, A. R. (1966) *Higher Cortical Functions in Man*. New York: Basic Books.

"Matt" (2001) Boing. Retrieved from www.telegraph.co.uk/comment/4262895/ Boing.html

Robertson, I. H. (1996) *Goal Management Training: A Clinical Manual*. Cambridge: PsyConsult.

Rylander, G. (1939) Personality changes after operation on the frontal lobes *Acta Psychiatrica Neurologica* Supplement No. 30.

Sacks, O. (1973) *Awakenings*. London: Duckworth and Co.

Shiozawa Wellness Center (n.d.) What is NSA? Retrieved from www.shioza-wawellness.com/what-is-nsa

Van Der Kolk, B. (2015) *The Body Keeps the Score: Mind, Brain, Body in the Transformation of Trauma*. New York: Penguin Random House.

Walker, M. (2017) *Why We Sleep: The New Science of Sleep and Dreams*. London: Penguin Books.

Watson, G. (n.d.) Pesticides? You decide. www.riverford.co.uk/pesticides-you-decide-systemic

WHO (World Health Organization) (2016) *Statistical Classification of Diseases and Related Health Problems*, 10th revision. Geneva, Switzerland: WHO.

Wikiquote (n.d.) Hafez. Retrieved from https://en.wikiquote.org/wiki/Hafez

Wilson, B. A., Dhamapurkar, S. & Rose, A. (2016) *Surviving Brain Injury after Assault: Gary's Story*. Hove: Psychology Press.

Index

Page numbers in **bold** denote tables, those in *italics* denote figures.